Copyright © 2014

The African Goddess Writers Collective

Alisa Kuumba Zuwena
Ayele Kumari
Nia Yaa Nebhet
Tonya Freeman
Priestess Esi
Shante Duncan
Dail Chambers

Cover Art by
Alisa Kuumba Zuwena

Back cover picture of Gourd lamp used under creative commons license. Artist=Nurettin Taskaya Foto=Nurettin Taskaya Mersin-TURKEY http://www.sukabagi.com

ISBN-10: 1503225119
ISBN-13: 978-1503225114

1

About this Book...

The Magical Calabash came about from a simple idea on a Facebook group to pool together and share a little piece of their work with other women. The Calabash is a symbol of womanhood in Africa and reflects the entire world as being a calabash. Everything in it is a part of a sacred whole. The calabash is a metaphor for the womb and women. It is the place where magic happens in the ancient traditions. A number of different objects might be placed in the calabash to create something new. Mysterious and ancient, this symbol speaks to what is offered in this book. It is a number of offerings for the pot of ancestral wisdom for women of African descent.

Each author is independent and her writing is hers alone. It does not reflect whole or in part anyone else's opinions or understanding of the topic. We simply gather together to tell our stories, share a little of what we have learned, and allow us all to grow from the process.

We hope you, the reader, can take our offerings and use them for years to come on your life's journey. Feel free to take what you need and we give thanks for the opportunity to share.

Ayele Kumari and the African Goddess Collective

Contents

3

4

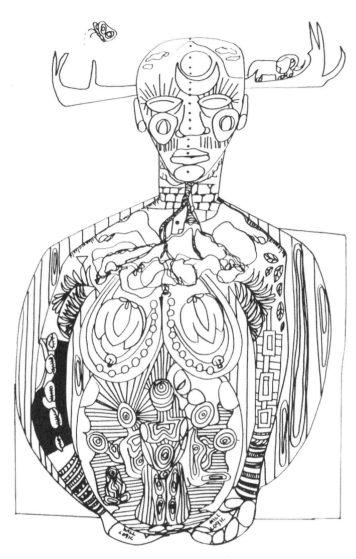

Primordial

by Dail Chambers

1 THE VOICE OF THE ANCESTORS

by Kuumba Zuwena

Love, willpower, support, feminine flowing energy and connecting with ancestral roots can be very powerful healing. I've been blessed to see and have a strong connection to the ancestors. Simply put, I can see and hear those who have passed on. This connection has led to profound healing, has shaped the course of my life, and has helped me help thousands of others.

In Detroit, during the 60's, my family lived on the Westside in 4 Family flat. We had a neighbor, by the name of Ruby. She had fish frys, and card games on Friday evenings. We all looked forward to this. Ruby had a sister by the name of Ruth. She was full of joy and a lively woman. She was a hairdresser at a shop on Davison near Dexter Avenue. She would often come to these gatherings. We were all very excited when Ruth became pregnant. She gave birth to a beautiful daughter that winter. Not long after the birth, she returned to work. Too quickly many felt. One day Ruth went outside with just a sweater to smoke a cigarette in the dead of winter and caught pneumonia. About three days later Ruth was dead. When I got the news, I was very sad and afraid of death. I cried and shouted, "I don't want to die".

During the funeral, friends and family of Ruth, walked past the open casket to say your goodbye. I was encouraged to do the same. I was terrified. I walked past her and saw her laying there. She appeared to be in a peaceful sleep.

That evening, Ruth visited me in the same dress she had been buried in. The lovely light blue satin sixties style form fitting dress. She sat at the end of my bed. I covered my head hoping that when I took the covers down; she would disappear or go back where she came from. But each time I took a look, she was still sitting there.

Ruth spoke to me. She told me not to worry about her, she was doing fine. She told me death was a natural occurrence. I had nothing to fear. She told me she would stay with me until I fell asleep. I eventually fell asleep.

The next morning, I looked for her everywhere. But, I never saw her again. What did happen though is that I began to have prophetic dreams about people before they made their transition to the other side. After the experience with Ruth, I had opened a doorway to the other side. My first sign of this was with my sister's godmother, Mrs. Robinson. My brother Duane and I loved her as if she was our godmother. I dreamed of her making her transition one Sunday morning.

As I was dreaming, she was having a heart attack in church. I told everyone about the dream and it scared them. Mrs. Robinson's heart attack was severe. She did not live to long after that Sunday. She transcended within a few months.

That experience made me fearful of telling anyone about dreams of that sort. I had not grown enough to realize that we are always transcending and changing. That it was the natural order of life. After all, we are spirit beings and the spirit lives.

It was a few years before I became more confident and secure in letting someone know of what I dreamt or saw in the spirit in reference to the other side. I came to understand that ancestors have a way of guiding, protecting and helping us.

Many times before someone passes, their spirit will visit me in my dream state to let me know they are crossing over. Many times they also leave messages for loved ones for me to deliver and I do. I think this happens sometimes because there are words and information that loved ones need to hear to have peace of mind and resolve. Also, it's very helpful for the necessary release process, tears. In many traditions, tears are the cleansing that is necessary for guiding the spirit and healing those left in this realm. The more tears, the more healing takes place.

It's very important to remember those who came before us. We are they, and they are us. We stand on the shoulders of our ancestors and we link them to the future. Many times we know and do things that we have not trained for or learned in school. Many times this is old energy, ancestral energy that is a part of you. A lot of times we are helping to work out karma for ourselves and for our ancestors as well.

I began to pursue my spiritual life in the late seventies. At that time, I did not connect the ancestors with any spiritual endeavors I was involved in. I began reading tarot cards in the 1981 and continued to grow and stretch in many directions. I became very clairvoyant and at times audio clairvoyant.

I moved to New York in 1986 to pursue my artistic career. I was able to perform and do many wonderful things. I also developed and met many people who vibrated at a very high spiritual level and their light was like a key for me; opening doors and revealing to me gifts that I never dreamed that could be channeled through me. One interesting story is with a man named Leonard Byrd. I met Leonard at a performing arts space in Brooklyn.

A group of some of my friends and myself who had spiritual gifts as well as artistic gifts got together and did a show and shared our spiritual gifts after. Leonard requested a tarot card reading from me at the time. During the reading he asked me about his health. He asked me to look at him and see if there were any problems. I told him I could not do that. He said very firmly, yes you can. And guess what, his body lit up in my mind like an x-ray. I could see he had some problems in the stomach area that were pretty serious. He told me afterward, what I had described was very accurate. So, after that day, I learned I could see health issues.

During the nineties, my gift to see the ancestors really flourished? My Ancestors had always been there. I found the key, when doing a chant I learned from a friend, who connected to the other side with Kemetic chants. The chant I did often during those days dealt with universal forces of wisdom from the old ones, the grandmother and grandfather energy. The ancestors as well as spirit guides began to come to me. They gave me all sorts of knowledge and messages for myself and others.

During the last few years, I discovered honoring them by pouring libation, as they do in many cultures in Latin America and African countries, was very empowering. Saying their names aloud and thanking them for the gift of life, the gifts of skills, knowledge from those who preceded you was very powerful and very helpful. It allowed me to understand certain karma families carry through generations. It enlightened me on why certain behaviors exist in your person you don't understand. The most powerful way for me to make contact comes through song/chants sung during their lifetime. There are instances when I will hear and sing tones that are just effective as the songs.

In 1997, I met a woman from New Orleans. Her name was Mama Jean Taiwo. Mama Jean, and she was a world renowned Healer/Spirit Worker, from New Orleans. She taught me that healing is most successful when the whole group involved participates. She also advised that when I work with the ancestors, I need 100% help from everyone participating. Before knowing this, I would carry the energy for many people and would feel exhausted for days after doing ceremonies. Now I require participation from the group when I host a ritual.

Everyone is blessed with a special gift. Some of us feel we have no power or anything special to offer in a healing situation. They are giving their power away when they think, feel and verbalize these thoughts. Sometimes, there is one person in the group who may have very nurturing and mothering qualities. These qualities are very important and necessary. There is nothing like the love of a mother.

In 1996, a good example of total group participation occurred on the beautiful and mystical St. Helena's Island, SC. The hanging moss on century old trees, the marshes, and sweet smells from the foliage in the area, and the very strong ancestral presence, provided the perfect atmosphere, for the powerful healing that took place that day. Four healings took place that day.

One particularly funny incident involved an 80 yr. old woman. She was experiencing pain in her legs and knees. After the healing circle, she began to dance. We couldn't stop laughing as we watched her feet move at what seemed to be 100mph. Another woman in her early thirties had explained to everyone, she was feeling back pain. She said she had been experiencing continuous pain. It had been going on for almost two months. After prayers, she was able to dance pain free. The biggest blessing of the day for everyone was clarity and a knowing.

The ability to communicate with the ancestors can help others directly and indirectly. A few years ago, I had a client who had been diagnosed with cancer. She was told she had about 3 months to live. During our session, I contacted her ancestors. They gave me a lot of information. She would have to be disciplined and diligent. They told me it was not her time to make a transition. After she left, my human side was terrified for her. I thought of her all night and prayed for her good health. She was the mother of two children. She was a very kind and sweet woman.

After our consultation, she changed her diet, had chemotherapy, and saw a woman known for her "laying on hands" healing abilities. Two years later, she was healthy and cancer free.

Around 2005, I joined The Trail of Dreams Walkers on the Appalachian Trails. The Trail of Dreams was a global walk for peace led by its visionary Audri Scott. The peace walk led a small group across the entire globe in an effort to promote peace among nations. It started by walking the path of the Trail of Tears, the path Cherokee people walked as they left their ancestral land for the reservations. I participated in a small leg at the beginning of what would become literally a walk across the world.

We arrived in Hot Springs and the campsite was

beautiful. It was next to the river. We set up our tents and had sandwiches and snacks that evening. We tried very hard to get the campfire going but all we could get was a flicker. We assumed it was because of the dampness coming from the river.

After eating, we sang to the ancestors. We sang old church songs and Native-American chants. The more sincere the prayers and song the more powerful are the results of this kind of sacred circle. Non-believers have had a change of heart after this type of spiritual work because of the blessings and interesting happenings that come forth. The blessings and info that comes forth is private intimate or only info that a someone who has transcended knows about the person. A very powerful Native American Healer came thru that evening, Mountain Eagle Woman. The Trail of Dreams had been her vision. After her messages and blessings of love and warmth, we went to bed.

The next morning, many of us had a lot to talk about. After we all went to sleep, or let's say tried to go to sleep. The campgrounds had come alive that night. The fire was ablaze. We kept hearing laughter and conversation, but whenever we would look out of our tents, we would see nothing. Dee-Dee informed us that while walking down the road, she heard footsteps behind her.

She thought one of us was playing with her. She turned her flashlight upon what she thought was somebody and to her surprise they disappeared... We all laughed at this phenomenon. The ancestors had a party as we attempted to sleep that night by the river. After all those events, we had a circle of healing and discussed what had taken place. The ancestors blessed us with a lot of healing and emotional release that morning.

The ancestors have also guided me these past few years and healed me also. In November 1999, a group of powerful spiritual folk gathered at my home one evening. Mama Jean was visiting and doing spiritual work here in Atlanta.

The ancestors came through several of the participants during the healing ritual. The very next day I was called by Emory Hospital for a kidney transplant. Yes, I had been on dialysis for 5 years before that special week.

The love of family and friends and most importantly the ancestors healed me. The god-mother-father energy and the ancestors carried me through those years with the spirit and allowed me luxuries with my poor health other dialysis patients never experienced. I traveled to Senegal, Africa. I went camping and did manual peritoneal dialysis in the

Rocky Mountains in Colorado and many other wonderful experiences. The ancestors held me up, as they can hold all of us on their shoulders.

To remember and honor our ancestors can enhance and empower your life in ways you can't imagine. When we forget them, they cannot help us. It's like a tree without roots, it dies. When we remember and keep their spirit alive the results are limitless and powerful.

Mermaids and Butterflies
By Alisa Kuumba Zuwena

2 Dreamweaving

By Ayele Kumari, PhD

I was in the bathtub playing in the bubbles when I felt my tooth get loose. I placed my finger on it to determine if it was ready to come out. I thought it funny that I had not been aware of a loose tooth. Still, it wiggled and then suddenly, it was out. I had wiggled my tooth free and placed it on the side of the tub on a deep purple rug. Excited, I knew that it would produce a dollar for me if I put it under my pillow. Reaching over to see it again, it turned to a pile of chicken bones on that purple rug. Perplexed, I awakened. I was 6 or 7 years old and that was the first of hundreds of dreams about my teeth coming out and my journey into the dreamtime.

Dreams are the portal through which we are able to understand ourselves and the inner worlds. The inner world consists of our mind, body, its components, as well as, other realms and the spiritual world. When we close our eyes, we are still able to "see" through our inner eye. Have you ever wondered when you close your eyes and have a dream or see a memory, what is doing the work of seeing it? It is this eye, also called the third eye, that we experience the visions coming through. This third eye is associated with the pineal gland in the brain. This inner eye is also where the experience of clairvoyance and psychic abilities come from. The inner eye, engaged through different states of consciousness, create this point of contact and communication from what is collectively known as the spiritual realm. Sort of like a piece of paper and pen for writing a letter, a dream can conceptualize a message using the language of interactive symbols. Like pen and paper, it can be used to record information, share information, brainstorm ideas, sooth comfort, inspire, etc.

Language of Dreams

Dreams use symbolic language to help us see what is taking shape in our lives. Dream work is powerful in that, through our dreams, we have the opportunity to interact with our Spirit without the limitations of preconceived ideas. It bypasses your awakened mind and deals directly with the sub and super conscious mind. While some dreams allow for your conscious interaction, most dreams are purely unconscious interactions between our personality and our Spirit. The mind creates archetypes through characters in our dreams. An archetype is a symbolic core principle or personality expressed as a person. These archetypes can then represent parts of us. For instance, if you have a parent that was a disciplinarian, you may still dream of that parent in your dreams in issues that require your discipline or direction. Like the outer archetypes, it is intended to give you a more objective view of what is going on with you. It is often difficult to clearly see ourselves because we are bias to our own views. When we can see them show up in a dream or in our worlds or even in our outer world and fully embrace that this is our own reflection that we are seeing, then we can see and understanding what our spirit is trying to show us.

We should understand that dreams do not use the same social, political standards or judgments that our outer world does. That is to say that its messages can show up in the most unusual ways. For instance, if you are in conflict about something in your life, it could show up as a bloody war or a violent episode in your dreams. The dream is not intending to show judgment about the thing so much as to show you what is happening inside in a clearly graphic way. So, there are no good or bad dreams except for how we judge and interpret them based on our experience of them. Likewise, if you are wan to meet someone or connect with someone, you may have a dream that you are kissing or intimately involved. It is not intended to be taken literally, but as a symbol of making a connection.

The Magical Dream World

Traditional and indigenous science held dreams to be a very important tool to receive guidance personally and for the community. It was common practice worldwide to map out the dream world to better navigate its realms and classify the guidance given. While different cultures call these world different things and may vary how they classify dream worlds, most can be placed within the context of 3 basic worlds. The upper, middle, and lower worlds or realms will include ancestral worlds, animal worlds, archetypal worlds, and higher selves, angels, deities, etc.

Understanding the dream world requires an understanding of other realms. Everything that comes into being in this material realm first comes through the more subtle realms. Everything exists on multiple dimensions. When we experience dreams, we could be tapping into a variety of dimensions or realms from the realm of our immediate mind to the realm of the great mind or spirit. Each realm has different qualities and characteristics of expressing in a dream. Recognizing those qualities can help you to better understand where the dream is coming from and the type of message or purpose it has. A few of the dream worlds are mentioned below along with its characteristics.

Ancestral Dream World

The ancestral world is the world immediately beyond the material world. This is the realm that the spirit passes through when one dies or crosses over. This realm is expansive and can involve ancestors on a variety of realms. The term ancestor itself is broad in that it is a lump term for many indigenous cultures to describe spiritual beings. There are, however, different kinds of ancestors and they will show up in a dream according to their soul's I progress on the other side. For instance, ancestors such as your Aunt May who just crossed over and had difficulties in her recent life, will come across differently than a distant ancestors who was a priestess. Just because a person has crossed over, does not mean that they are suddenly enlightened and know everything. They can always be helpful as they were when they were living. They may also be limited in their understanding of your soul's purpose even on the other side due to their limited exposure there. When soul's die, they continue to grow as they continue to exist. They may also progress through many different realms in their journey before they are settled.

I discovered this when my father crossed over. Each dream he came to me, he was in a different space and carried different qualities as time when on. When he had just crossed over, he was hurried and a little younger. He was trying to make amends for some of the issues he had created while on earth. He was hurried but made it clear that he heard my calls and he was here. He gave me messages for my mother. He was still bound by time in some form.

One of my most memorable ancestral dreams was when I was wanting a family heirloom and I asked my father about it. He showed up in my dream with a white plastic bag. In that bag was a bunch of junk jewelry, but also something with an eagle on it. He told me it was mine if I wanted it. I thought it was something from the military since he was in the Army. He said that it was in Sandy's house on the right side of the bed where he slept. After years, I wasn't sure if it was there, but I went to Sandy's house and into the room where he slept. On the right side of the bed, there was a table and under the table a safe. Upon opening the safe, there was a white bag, with a lot of junk, and... a gold pendant with a eagle on a cross. I had forgotten that he had worn it. It was, however, a clear sign that he had communicated with me from the other side since no one, including Sandy, knew it was there!

As the dreams with him progressed, my father appeared on a bright and sunny farm where he had grown up. He was in a state of peace then. Relaxed and comfortable, I could see that he was in a state of recovery. He, along with my Uncle Jim hugged me and told me they loved me. They also gave me advice on my marriage. Uncle Jim, who was very much like my husband when he lived, was particularly helpful. He even smelled like the cherry tobacco he smoked in his pipe when he was alive. I was lucid and very clear that they were on the other side. Even later, I saw dad again and he was very tall and glowing. I understood instinctively that he had crossed yet another realm. He was not as interested in things of this realm although he was still there for us. Seeing this transition in my dreams over time helped me to understand the different realms and how ancestors can show up. I have also experienced this phenomenon many times with others and other relatives who have crossed over.

Ancestors from the etheric realms or just transitioning over tend to appear as they had when they were alive. Often, they revert fairly early to a younger appearance. It seems to be a world that mimics our world. They are still with those we know as family. The dreams tend to be geared toward family issues and concerns. They retain the same personalities and belief systems they had when they were on this side. From Christian to Native American, to ancient African, they are able to speak and share information about their belief. They have the same religious preferences and cultural perceptions. My distant ancestors from the Ga-Dangbe in Ghana and East Africa show up differently and with different preferences than my more immediate ancestors. In fact, they are the ones who gave me my current name. My first name, Ayele, is from the ones from Ghana and the last name Khu Mari is from the East African side.

Forces of nature also live in the etheric realm and can be impacted to impact weather and nature in the material realm. Animal spirits can communicate with us here as well. If we dream in this realm, a lot of our immediate thoughts, fears, and emotions are experienced here. In some ways, we exist in both realms simultaneously.

The next noticeable realm of ancestral dreams is when they begin to appear a little distant. This is considered the astral realm. They have detached from the material realm and no longer concerned so much with mundane earthbound affairs. Or they may be more community and globally focused rather than on a individual. These are considered the elevated ancestors. They may have transcended the need to incarnate or they may have attained some level of mastery. This world seems to involve not just beings who were once a part of your immediate family, but those who are also your spiritual guides and a part of your soul family. This kind of ancestral dream may show up through symbols or recurrent phrases and may involve information from past lives, and alternate lives. They may give you a message and look like someone else. This is where the message is more important and their ego of needing to be seen a certain way is not there.

This world may also involve other types of beings that we don't always recognize on earth as fairies, dragons, and large birds and other beings. You may fly to other worlds in this realm and through the astral planes. This realm is very vivid. The colors are vivid in this realm...like brilliant light. Once you are traveling through this realm, you will encounter a number of beings that may change form directly in front of you. Your understanding of the world will be greatly enlarged after having experienced this world.

The last type of ancestral dream realm is when they appear as tall ethereal beings. This may not be the case all of the time. They have transcended completely our realm and are back fully in the spiritual realm. They usually appear as 8 feet tall or more and have a glow to them. The tall stature is not really noticeable in the dream...only in retrospect when waking. Here, the interest and messages are involving your soul's journey and the global welfare of the planet are prevalent. There is a tendency in this realm, to hear music. In fact, there is often a message with music in the background. The music is often very beautiful and moving. Sometimes it is a popular song, but the message is important for you to pay attention to. From these realms, there seem to be watchers or our higher selves. Here, the language of symbols take on new importance and are used to convey great messages.

Other dream worlds involve the archetypal worlds. This is the world is very abstract and is the world where we experience deities and blueprint of the world we live in. This is the creative world where things begin to come into being. Dreams from this realm will be highly symbolic and will involve large groups of symbols for ideas. These are dreams describing the Great Spirit and messages from the greater spiritual realm.

Other types of people who show up in your dreams may also be symbolic. Often the Spirit may use others in your waking life to represent someone or something in your dream state. The zodiac sign or name can give a clue as to who it might represent. For instance, I almost never get a name directly. Often if a name is given, I need to take the first letter of the name to represent who it is talking about. I may hear Rita in a dream and the person might be Rebecca. Or the person in the dream may have a sun sign in Aquarius and it represents a person who is an Aquarius. Sometimes you have to search a little to understand how the dream is communicating.

Types of Dreams

In addition to the type of dream worlds we may journey to and experience, there are a variety of dream types that may also play a part in the dream message. While dreams can take us to other realities, dreams can also just happen in our individual minds. The first dream that we may have upon going to sleep is often such a dream. These types of dreams often catalog the day's experiences and file them for recall and reference. These dreams help us with memory of material and also to plant seeds that we want to manifest. Depending on what happened, it could take hours to file away the day's events. As a teacher, I have found that students tend to retain the lessons better if they review them before going to sleep. The information is taken into their sleep and it helps with retention.

Bedtime Practice

One way to get more message dreams and less cataloging is to review your day backwards before you go to bed. This acts as a cataloging and the mind accepts it as such. This can also help us to learn more about ourselves in the process. Once the cataloging is done, the mind is freer to explore new things in the dream state.

Other dreams that may occur during this time are dreams from your body's messengers. Every cell in your body has consciousness and communicates with every other cell. This communication can happen with you as well if you learn to tune in. Sometimes we may have a dream after eating something and we can see the effects of that food in our system. Other dreams may show us in a bathroom which may point to our elimination system or kidneys.

Navigating the Dream House

A big part of dream interpretation may involve dreams in which a regular house, family house, or the house you grew up in occurs. Dreams where you always find yourself in a certain house is usually a symbol of you. Each room in the house may represent different parts of you. I always dream about the house I grew up in. My childhood bedroom represents my innermost self. My kitchen is where I nourish myself. My parent's room is often my relationships. My family room is usually my family life. The living room is usually my spiritual life, etc. It may be different for each person, but learning how your spirit communicates in this house is important to good dream work.

Early morning dreams-

Dreams that happen in the morning are often dreams with messages and prophetic. After the mind has had time to process and the body is fully rested, messages begin to come through. People usually miss these messages because they wake to startling alarm clocks and immediately just get up and start their hectic day.

Early Morning Dream Practice:

Practice waking naturally or to very soft gentle music with no words. When you wake softly, try to maintain the rhythmic breathing pattern you had asleep. Pay attention to the natural sounds around you and quietly ask to recall your dreams. Then wait for impressions to come in.

Lucid Dreams

Lucid dreams happen when you become conscious in your dream state. That is, you become aware that you are in a dream or altered state and can interact with the characters in that altered state of consciousness. These dreams are the most memorable and exciting because they allow you to do and learn things that would be difficult to do or learn in your waking state. I often fly in my lucid dreams and go to different planets and star systems. When I first started this practice, I began to journey to the black hole. I found out it was a vortex long before scientist had discovered such. Other lucid dreams allowed me to visit people I had not seen in years. If you find yourself in a lucid dream, try to interact with the dream to stay in it. It is often difficult because the dreams gets overly excited and begins to waken. Interacting helps you to stay with the original sequence of the dream.

Visions

Visions and dreams come from the same place in the mind and are not that different. The work of the pineal gland is responsible for both. The level of consciousness or waking is usually the difference. Visions happen in a half sleep half wake state. These are also often what we see when we are in a very relaxed state or meditating. These dreams often allow us to ask questions and receive answers to situations in our lives. When we understand that our greater or Goddess Selves are always present and active, we can then realize that we never have to look far for guidance. It is a matter of learning to be still rather than a matter of looking everywhere. Visions are what happen in the stillness.

Shared or Community Dreaming

I became aware of shared or community dreaming while napping with a friend on the same couch. Both of us dosed off at the same time and had a brief but impactful dream. Upon waking, we found that we both dreamed of the same thing only we were different people in the dream. This helped me to understand that dreams are larger than just our small perceptions.

As my dream work continued, I developed dream partners. These were people with whom we regularly shared our dreams. Most mornings, I would wake and talk to one of them. We would then share and interpret each other's dreams. What we began to find is that we would have dreams about each other and sometimes have each other's dream. When one was too stressed, another would have the dream as if the character was them. We began to understand that the Spirit will speak through anyone who is most receptive and often through several if you notice the themes.

There is also a practice of community dreaming practiced in the indigenous cultures that took one person's dream and found what that dream meant for each person. As the dreams were shared, each person's dream brought up different messages for each person hearing it. For instance, if a person had a dream and shared it with Person A, B, C and D. A, B, C, and D would hear different things in the dream that mean something to them. The original dream had personal messages to person hearing it. Through sharing it, the dream was for the community. It could also point to greater community messages of issues family, or theirs that may need to be addressed.

Community Dream Practice

Connect with at least one other person who is interested in dream work. Allow them to become your dream partners by sharing each other's dreams and recording them. When listening to the dream, ask yourself what it could mean to them in their lives, but also what it could mean for you in your life. Regular practice can reveal powerful messages for each participating person and deepen your connection with them.

Epic Dreams

Epic dreams are those dreams with greater messages that are so powerful, you might wake up, write it down, go to the bathroom, then lay back down and it continues. They usually last a significant portion of the night if not all night and sometimes over days. Writing them down is key to understanding them. It may be explaining a process that is occurring or giving messages of what is to come. Whenever they happen, it is important to pay attention as it is intended to get your attention.

Sleep paralysis

This is not really a dream but often occurs and frightens people experiencing it. It happens when you wake up and you cannot move your body. What has occurred is that your soul, the part that animates your body has traveled and not returned yet to the body. The body woke up but the soul isn't fully joined again. This often happens with people who have over active minds and racing thoughts. It often occurs to individuals who find it hard to relax. When this happens, do not panic, but breathe deeply. The deep breaths will synchronize and movement with be restored.

How to Remember Your Dreams

Everyone dreams even if they cannot remember their dreams. The ability to remember dreams comes from a number of factors. First, the state of your parasympathetic nervous system can determine if you are able to remember dreams. This is the part of our nervous system that allows for rest and relaxation. If you are constantly engaged in outer activities, stress, and excessive mental activity, you may find more difficulty in remembering your dreams. To counter that, you need to incorporate regular times to fully rest completely. Eight hours a night plus regular meditation can help with that. Eight hours are important because I have found that my most memorable dreams are in the morning after I have fully slept through the night at least 6 to 7 hours of sleep. If I got adequate rest, then the next 2 hours will offer clearer dreams and messages from my Spirit. Your personal sleep quotient may be different so you may need to experiment with it to find what works for you.

Recording your dreams will begin to help you understand how your Spirit and spiritual world communicates with you and help you to remember them. Often, if we don't record them, we will forget them as the day goes on. I used to use a blank book to record my dreams, but now I use my iPad dream journal, and also I use my phone's voice recorder to verbally record the dream. My phones notes app also allows for quick notes in the middle of the night. Recording your dreams regularly sets up a spiritual practice that will allow you to better be in touch with your source. Because of this, dream books are only partially helpful. Most dream books are based on someone else's experiences of dreams and even their personal interpretation of the significance of events. Their experience may not necessarily reflect your own. It is because of this you may need to measure for yourself how meaningful an interpretation is for you. On the other hand, I have found that Spirit will communicate with you in any form you accept, so if you accept the meanings presented in the book, your

Spirit will utilize those symbols when appropriate. The Spirit is a dynamic living intelligence and is therefore quite capable of changing with what is needed to get a point across. In any case, I have included a Dream Journal Worksheet in this essay that can be copied so that several could be printed out and added to a dream binder or workbook.

How to Improve Your Ability to Dream

The ancients have long studied the types of things to do to improve your dreams. While you can order some dreams herbs from Africa or South America, there are other practical ways to improve your dreams right where you are. The number way that can help is simply staying properly hydrated. Water is a conduit for Spirit and our bodies are made up of 75% water. Dehydration or inadequate water intake can hinder your ability to fully remember your dreams. Water is a conduit for the Spirit and can help with receptivity. People who have a lot of water in their astrological chart or in their body often have clear dreams. Larger women with higher fat content or pregnant women often dreams more clear because the fat holds water in the body and allows for greater receptivity. Many African priestesses were often full figured and it allowed for them to channel spiritual messages and energies.

The ability to relax deeply can also play a large role. Meditation before sleep can help you to have a more relaxed night's sleep. Breathwork can also be helpful in remembering your dreams and relaxing. Steady consistent deep rhythms can often help with recall if you haven't produced too much movement. If you are mindful of the breathing pattern that you had upon waking and can mimic it, this will often bring the dream flooding back to your waking state.

Dream Supplements

Other things that may help in the process is the supplement choline or lecithin. These supplements help to nourish the parasympathetic nervous system and improve memory. They can also help to reduce fat in the liver as a side benefit but they should be taken with caution as too much choline can cause bloating and a slight body odor. These supplements are plentiful and can be obtained in a health food store and most drug stores. Other ways to get this nutrient can be through cabbage, eggs, soybeans, wheat germ.

Galantamine is another supplement that helps with increasing dreams and lucid dreaming. It has also been said to assist with dream recall as well. It comes from the red spider lily and the snowdrop plant. It has also been shown to be helpful with Alzheimer's as a side benefit. This particular supplement may be accompanied with a B complex to assist with nervous energy and should also be taken according to instructions which usually means that it should not be taken right before bedtime but earlier.

Dream Teas

Also there are herbal teas that can be helpful in producing clear dreams.

Dream Recipe 1

mugwart flower essence or herb - improves dream clarity and psychic ability

yarrow- provides spiritual protection from spirit world

basil , (prefer Holy Basil) improves dream quality and memory

lavender- calms mind to promote happier dreams

rosemary- improves mental clarity

Steep equal amounts of herbs for 20 minutes. Strain. Focus on a question or concern and drink before bedtime. Taking this tea before bedtime has produced wonderfully clear dreams for me.

Dream recipe number 2

valerian root
kava kava
chamomile

Use the same instructions as above.

Other supplements that demand special mention are 2 flower essences that have helped me greatly with dream recall and messages. Flower essences are not the same as essential oils. They have no scent and can be placed in drinking water or absorbed through the skin in a bath. Mugwart flower essence is one such essence. Another essence is a combination essence and is produced by Green Hope Farms. The essence combination "To Hear the Angels Sing" has produced phenomenal dreams for me.

Advanced Practices

The above are beginning practices that can help you to engage in active dream work right now. For the scope of this writing, these things should be understood and worked on prior to engaging in other practices. Advanced practices beyond these may be found in an upcoming book, "Birth of A Goddess" or in one of my facilitated workshops. These workshops can be found on my website, www.ayelekumari.com Practices such as dream divination, along with programming dreams are some advanced practices. Others, such as taking on case studies and dreams for healing still await you. For now, develop a regular dream practice, improve dream recall and explore.

Dream Journal Form

*Date*_____

*Time*_____

Describe the dream in as much detail as possible:

Identify specific colors, scents, songs, phrases, and items that stood out to you:

What major symbols come to mind from the dream?

What time period or frame was it set in?

What mood did the dream leave you with? Feelings?

What special characters were involved? If they were people that you know, what are their zodiac signs? Did they glow?

Dream Journal Form continued

Where they human, animal, other, or mixed?

What are the themes?

What special guidance or specific message can you identify in the dream?

What else is going on in your life or has been in the last few days/ weeks? Does it reflect anyone else's life that you are close to? Does there appear any relationship between the two?

What spiritual or cultural values do you place on the symbols or characters present in the dream?

What are your first impressions of the dream?

What is your intuition telling you or other alternative or possible meanings?

Dream Journal Form Continued

Other people's interpretations or perceptions?

Later Reflections over next days or weeks?

Has anything come to pass that was reflected in the dream?

3 Increasing Your Vibrations: How to Evolve w/ The Planet

by Priestess Esi, DM

What is all this talk about increasing vibrations? Why are some people so concerned with this concept? What does it actually mean to increase your vibration? How does all this tie into the Goddess? As you continue to read, you will see that I have a few mini-articles included to further explain this concept.

Well, stay in your seats. We are going to get into all of this and more! It is *my* absolute pleasure to take you on this interestingly informative journey into what increasing your vibration really means, *why* it is important and the "end" result of it all.

First of all, what are these "vibrations" I am talking about? In order to understand this subject from its core, we must investigate this term, "vibrations" first. According to the Merriam-Webster Dictionary, a vibration is a characteristic emanation, aura, or spirit that infuses or vitalizes someone or something and that can be instinctively sensed or experienced. It can also be described as a distinctive usually emotional atmosphere capable of being sensed. Have you ever walked into a room full of upset people and you felt those vibes before you even saw the physical evidence of it? We all vibrate on different levels and each level affects our consciousness.

Before I delve deeper, you might want to ask yourself these questions: Do I enjoy the state the world is currently in today? What can make things better? Why are there people fighting on "opposite" ends of every possible spectrum when it comes to religion, politics, sexual orientation, etc? Where do I fit in or belong in all of this? What is the meaning of this all? By the end of this article, you will have a deeper understanding of what it means to increase your vibrations and why it is so critical to do so at this time. You will see that in order to keep up with the changes that are currently going on, we must increase our vibrations to vibrate at the same frequency of Mother Earth!

Alright, you have waited long enough. Let us get straight into it. The definition of vibration that I mentioned above shows that vibrations can be *felt* and all vibrations are not the same. There are lower vibrations which we can relate to the lower chakras and higher vibrations which we can relate to the higher chakras. Chakras are wheels of energy that are located along the spinal column and they help to govern various behaviors; they represent various levels of consciousness within each human. Chakras are much more than this, but I gave the simple definition so that you can see how chakras fit into all of this. **Note: I will be using the terms, "higher chakras" and "higher self" interchangeably and likewise, "lower chakras" and "lower self" interchangeably as well.** The lower chakras govern safety, food, money, or anything to do with survival. Our lower chakras are based on ego and ego is ridden with fear. Fear about what we will eat, what we will wear, where we will live, are we safe, etc? Let us take a look at one of the scriptures in the Bible. *Note: You do not have to be a Bible follower to derive wisdom from it.* EVERYTHING consists of wisdom; we just need to know when to take what is beneficial to us and when to throw the rest away. Here is the scripture taken from the King James Bible which relates to our human concerns that stem from our lower self. *Luke 12:27-32: 27 Consider the lilies how they grow: they toil not, they spin not; and yet I say unto you, that Solomon in all his glory was not arrayed like one of these. 28 If then God so clothe the grass, which is today in the field, and tomorrow is cast into the oven; how much more will he clothe you, O ye of little faith? 29 And seek not what ye shall eat, nor what ye shall drink, neither be ye of doubtful mind . 30 For all these things do the nations of the world seek after : and your Father knoweth that ye have need of these things. 31 But rather seek ye the kingdom of God; and all these things shall be added* *unto you. 32 Fear not, little flock; for it is your Father's good pleasure to give you the kingdom.* It seems like it is normal for people to worry about such things. These things are tied to our survival. If we have no food, how can we survive? Now, observe the interesting statements concerning the, "Kingdom". What *is* this kingdom spoken about in this scripture? The Kingdom represents our higher self! Try to remember it this way; the Kingdom is within US (our higher self) and the crown chakra is a part of our higher self. The King or Queen wears a crown. The Kingdom, which resides in our higher self along with our crown chakra, has to do with our higher consciousness (increasing our vibrations) also known as our higher self. The higher self is connected to Divine Consciousness. Divine Consciousness is basically higher thinking; it relates to thinking about things that go deeper than just what we look like, what we will eat, where we will live and the like. If you can understand this simple equation, you will be able to keep up with the rest of this article: Lower Self (*lower frequency*) = Physical Concerns whereas Higher Self (*higher frequency*) = Spiritual Concerns. Divine Consciousness is held in our crown chakra which is where the Kingdom resides!

Let us get back to the scripture above that describes human fears. Fear is not necessarily a bad thing (it actually helps with our survival), but fear is something that has to be let go of as we increase our vibrations and move from lower to higher chakras. Our higher chakras do not consist of fear-based thoughts (that is key). Higher chakras are not connected to survival. Our higher chakras (higher self) can be activated once the needs of the lower chakras are already satisfied. Think of it like this; who wants to meditate while they are hungry and in fear of their physical safety? You won't be able to concentrate! It is much easier to meditate when your body is properly nourished and you are in a safe and secure dwelling. Fear is something that should only be used for our survival; it should NOT be used to cripple us. *Note: There is a mini-article coming up ahead that I think you will enjoy and it explains why we have fear and how it ties in with survival.* Our higher chakras govern our connection to spirit, intuition, the universe and higher thinking. The lower chakras are more concerned with, "I" and "Me" whereas the higher chakras are concerned with, "WE". I will be hitting on various mini-topics in order to explain the concept of increasing our vibration in a clear, concise manner. My aim is to put all of my thoughts together in a way that can easily be understood. I am going to move on to discussing what it means to crawl before you walk in a mini-article I created and then I will tie that back into what I was discussing in my previous pages. This is only a small portion of the puzzle.

Mini-Article I

Crawl Before Walk

We must crawl (as animals do) before we walk (as gods/goddesses do).

When animals crawl, they have a closer connection to Mother Earth (all of their limbs make contact with the earth when they walk) and with this close contact, their natural instincts are better kept intact. Allow me to dissect this concept even further for a moment. When we are babies, are we not true to our instincts? Did not we cry when we needed food or attention? It is very interesting that children learn to crawl first (as animals do) before walking. This shows we must first learn all we can from our lower "animalistic" selves before we can move into our higher self (true divinity). When a child is born, he/she does not walk out of his/her mother's womb. There are various stages of development that we all had to go through in order to make it to the next phase. Crawling is symbolic of our lower, instinctual selves and walking represents our god/goddesshood which is connected to our higher self.

Out of all the beings on this planet, who hurts and destroys the earth the most? Ding, ding, DING!!!! You said it! WE do! Consider this; we are the ones walking upright, correct? In the paragraph above, I mentioned that animals have a strong physical connection to the earth because most of them crawl which allows more of their limbs to make contact with Mother Earth, but wait, we do not have such a physical connection as the animals do. Animals even get their foods directly from the earth or they eat other animals that get their foods directly from the earth. They are herbivores (fed directly by Mother Earth), carnivores (fed by animals that are fed directly by Mother Earth), omnivores (fed by Mother Earth and by animals that are fed directly by Mother Earth), or scavengers (fed by the dead animals that lay upon Mother Earth). The human experience is very different because our foods are store-bought and badly processed. No wonder we have forgotten our connection to Mother Earth! Not only this, but we literally walk with our heads in the air as if we are somehow higher than the earth. You see? Our heads are in the clouds; we are too high up on ourselves. We need to humble ourselves and regain that connection with Mother Earth. We have allowed our upright position to somehow feed us the illusion that we are not a part of the earth and that we are somehow higher. How can one be higher than the place that feeds him/her? That is completely absurd! We need to reconnect to Mother Earth, but that does not mean we have to *physically* crawl; we need to go outside and get to understand Mother Nature and all of the creatures that live among us better. Accept your lower instincts to obtain food, sex and territory. There is nothing shameful about these instincts because they are necessary for survival. Please know that you have the instinct to kill when threatened. That is for YOUR benefit and the benefit of your loved ones. In reality, sometimes it is either "us" or "them" and it is surely not going to be "us". Do not fool yourself into thinking you are somehow above defending and caring yourself. Your first requirement to live on this planet is to be able to know how to STAY ALIVE; that is basic and this ability resides in our lower chakras (lower self). That is why the lower self is so important. It helps us to remain alive. We have to remain alive in order to carry out our *higher* purpose. How can we move into higher thinking when we have not yet understood the importance of lower instincts? Understand that the "animal" is inside of you. Realize that there is a rhythm and flow to nature and we are a part of that rhythm and flow. We cannot walk before we crawl! ***We must be aware of how our lower self operates and how it benefits us before we graduate to our higher self.***

When we finally reconnect to the earth and her inhabitants, we will better understand ourselves and we can then walk the face of the earth as true gods and goddesses because WE will understand ourselves (our lower and higher self). We will know that in order for us to be taken care of, we need to take care of Mother Earth first. That is imperative. What do you think will happen when she gets tired of our nonsense?

Thankfully, there is still time to make a change and the more people understand and apply these concepts, the better it will be for all of us!

I am going to be painstakingly clear; **do not** fear your lower instincts. We have to understand and properly manage our lower self before moving up to our higher self. There is nothing "high" or "mighty" about ruining the earth now is there? We are the ones causing damage to our environment. Let us get back to the root of who we are starting from our lower self (lower chakras) and what is interesting about this idea is that the chakra that relates to survival is called the "root chakra". Go down to your root chakra and work your way up! You have to start low first (crawl) before you can walk. We are *looking* the part of gods and goddesses (walking upright), but we sure are not acting the part.

This concept of crawling before walking can be used to describe many things and one thing in particular that it can describe is that we must not neglect our bodies for our spirits, but care them equally. After all, how can we complete our purpose on this earth while our bodies are sickly or dead? The physical body is a tool used by our spirit to complete our life purpose! We must take care of our bodies so that they can be around for the duration of our mission. This is yet another example of maintaining balance with our lower and higher self.

Reconnect with Mother Earth and let her Wisdom teach you what it really means to be human. You will then be better prepared to evolve with her because you are starting at a stage of infancy, but do not let that discourage you because infants grow and mature rapidly.

After Thoughts
<u>The meaning of "Crawl Before Walk" and how it ties into Increasing Our Vibrations:</u>

The above post was written to show that before we go higher in vibrations, we must get down low in order to remember our roots and to re-establish who we are, why we are here and how we fit into our environment as a whole. We cannot graduate high school until we have successfully completed elementary-styled learning. We cannot, in a balanced fashion, move from lower to higher self without first learning what we need to learn from our lower self. There are too many people fumbling around and tripping over each other because they are attempting to walk before crawling. This is one reason why our world is currently out of balance and out of touch which has led to our being out of our minds. **Fortunately, at the end of this article will be exercises that you can implement in order to help you get back in step with the ever-evolving vibration of Mother Earth!**

I hope you enjoyed the mini-article concerning crawling before walking. I would like to discuss fear and how this plays a role in our lower self (which aids survival) and why it is important to make a distinction between survival-based fears and crippling, unusual fears. When fear is maintained in its rightful place, you can evolve with the vibrations of the earth, but if your fear gets out of hand, it can stunt your growth.

Mini-Article II

Fear

Is fear a bad thing? Not necessarily. Fear is an emotion that normal humans and even animals possess for their survival. When you think of, "fight or flight", that is in reference to fear. Fear is meant to aid us in the area of survival and is associated with our root chakra; the root chakra governs survival. The interesting thing is that there is a strong link between the root chakra and adrenal glands. The adrenal glands are equipped to elicit the,"fight or flight" response. Do you see how all of these elements tie in? Let me give an example of the root chakra, fear and adrenal glands working together to provide protection for the possible "victim" of a threat.

If you have ever heard gunshots going off, your immediate reaction may be to duck, fall flat on the ground or run. *That* **is the appropriate reaction to**

such a situation and this reaction is rooted in fear. The adrenal glands became activated once a possible threat was recognized. The adrenal glands have a strong connection to the root chakra and the root chakra is connected to survival and the lower self. Another example is if a person is trying to attack you; the response to defend yourself and fight back is quite normal and it can allow you to remain alive. Imagine seeing someone get attacked and they just stood there staring into space; you would assume they were mentally ill. Fear is an emotion that can be triggered instantly, and in the same manner, can disappear immediately. When the adrenal glands are activated, it causes us to get a quick burst of extra energy and faster thinking ensues. Fear is necessary, but *only* when it aids in our survival.

Now, let me explain how fear should NOT be used. Fear should NOT be experienced over long periods of time. Does the fear of public speaking fall into the category of survival? No, it does not! Many of us have suffered with this fear, but it is an unusual fear and it does not aid in our survival; in fact, it is a crippling fear that is illogical. In my opinion, this sort of fear is a learned behavior. I am almost certain that a 9 month old baby would have no problem speaking in front of a crowd. Well, the baby would be babbling, but babbling confidently with no fear! Unfortunately, by the time the baby becomes an adolescent and has reached the age of around 12, he/she would possibly have acquired the same fear that many others have acquired. Now let us get back to why such a fear is illogical and has nothing to do with survival. Anything is possible, but is it likely that you would get killed during a speech? I do not think so, and even if this were to happen, your fear of speaking in front of others was not rooted in your own physical safety; it was rooted in making a fool of yourself. Everyone has played the fool at one point or another and appearing foolish in front of others does not warrant our demise. Those who fear public speaking fear how they will sound and how others will view them. Does that fear make sense? There is no link between public humiliation and death. Public speaking does not threaten your life so why entertain that fear? This sort of fear does not protect your life, but instead, it hampers your life. Some people have ongoing, illogical fears that serve no purpose for their survival. If fearful thoughts linger in your mind, you are experiencing long lasting fear that is not logical in the realms of survival. These fears cannot protect your life, but they can definitely drain the life force from you!

Do you know what happens in the body when the "fear response" is turned on? Adrenaline is released into the bloodstream and causes the following to occur:

- Your heart rate increases to pump more blood to your muscles and brain to allow you to think and react faster.
- You nerve cells begin to shoot off.
- Lungs take air in faster in order to supply your body with more oxygen.
- The pupils in your eyes become larger to increase the scope of your eyesight.
- Various organ systems that do not help you fight or flee slow down for the moment so you can concentrate on surviving an attack on your life.

To prepare for fight or flight, your body does these things automatically so it can be ready for quick action or a quick escape. If you are speaking in front of others, is there really a logical need to escape or flee? That sounds funny, does it not? Of course it does because it is not a logical fear that is used for SURVIVAL. I am sure that the fear that results in speaking in front of a crowd is not as intense as the fear that results in being faced with a murderer, but you get my drift. Fear, even on a small scale, has an effect on the body. Why put your body through this needlessly? It is obvious that the fear-response to a real attack is powerful enough to protect us, but let us not waste our adrenal glands on illogical fears. The more illogical fears we have, the more our bodies react as if we are in a 'fight or flight" situation and this leads to the body becoming stressed. What is the result of stress? It is disease.

Be balanced. Fear is good for survival situations but let us not allow this emotion to affect other areas of our lives. Do not worry because we all have illogical fears to contend with; at the end of this article will be little tips and tricks to overcome some of these fears. **It is important to keep your survival instincts intact while eliminating illogical fears.**

After Thoughts
The meaning of "Fear" and How it Ties into Increasing Our Vibrations:
The above post was written to show that fear is necessary for our survival and is rooted in our lower self (which is needed), but can become a nuisance when we allow that emotion to invade other areas of our lives.

The next mini-article explains what is going on right now on earth and possibly even the Universe. Duality is increasingly becoming non-existent at this time. Read on.

Mini-Article III

The Veils are Coming Down

"Good" verses "evil", life verses death, health verses sickness, right verses wrong, up verses down, left verses right, chaos verses order, etc. They ALL stem from the same Source! In times past, people tried

60

to create the illusion that these concepts were somehow distinctly different and separate from each other, but in reality, they all work together. The veils are coming down because the lines between each "opposite" concept are becoming blurry. Without an opposite reaction, how can we grow? Just imagine if the Universe was only "good" and there was no suffering, death, disease or the like. There would be no room for evolution. If there is no room for evolution, everything will always stay the same. If everything stayed the same, what goal can be reached? NONE!

Everyone wants to be unique from everyone else and base how they perceive themselves in comparison to others just by these concepts such as "good" and "evil", etc. Why do all of these "things" exist together? They are from the same Source. In the next mini-article, I would like to discuss that every single thing that we experience is important to our survival and to our evolution. We can only go so far in increasing our vibrations if we do not understand this simple concept. I call this mini-article "The Supreme". Understanding the Supreme at the basic core will assist in building a strong foundation to increase our vibrations. Enjoy!

Mini-Article IV

The Supreme

All of us are an aspect within the Supreme Being who is the All in All within All. As humans, we tend to perceive things in opposites. EVERYTHING that YOU ARE is a part of the Supreme Being because NOTHING resides from without the Supreme (the Supreme is EVERYTHING and in EVERYONE). Some see the Supreme as being "God" or "Goddess" but I see much more! The Supreme SURPASSES gender, good vs evil; light vs dark, life vs death, peace vs war. The SUPREME is all of that and more. There are certain aspects of the Supreme that we all are not too fond of and to remedy this distaste for certain aspects of the Supreme, we attempt to overcome the guilt of not loving all there is in the Supreme by creating a "devil" or a "Supreme Evil One" to label as "The Enemy". We label the 'not-so-comfy' aspects of the Supreme as the devil. Yes, there are adversaries, but not in the way a lot of people see "them". In order to grow, we need a force that appears to be an opposing force to fight against and when we fight, we say it is the opposite force of the Supreme. There is NO opposite force of the Supreme; it IS the Supreme you are fighting against, but that is fine because the Supreme loves a good fight! The Supreme knows it makes us stronger. If there was an opposing force outside of the Supreme, the Supreme would not be the Supreme. Take a moment to read Isaiah 45:7. It explains that the god of the Bible formed the light and created the darkness; he claims making peace and also war, he says he creates good and also evil and the scripture ended with his declaring, "I do all of these things." Even the god of the Bible is an *aspect* of the Supreme. Let me repeat, "the god of the Bible is an *aspect* of the Supreme; The Supreme is much too extensive to even be captured in a book, but this passage in Isaiah brings forth the message that I am trying to convey to you that any being who claims to be the one who has created all things has created ALL things (even unpleasant things). Who is without the Supreme? No one! All these things that we call angels, demons, sickness, death, life, health, and the like are ALL different aspects of the Supreme; they just vibrate at different frequencies and all of them are necessary. Even if they are not all desired, they are definitely necessary. Medicine does not always taste or feel good.

Even within you, your demons are an aspect of the Supreme and you have a right to not "vibe" with that aspect at that time, but they are there for a reason and if they cause discomfort, it is because there is something you are not allowing yourself to learn. Do I love every aspect of the Supreme? NO! No way! Why? I do not love every aspect of the Supreme because the Supreme encompasses every single thing whether "good" or "bad". Good and bad are LESSONS and no one loves every lesson they receive. Even within yourself, there are aspects you are not fond of, but they are there for a reason and IS a part of the Supreme Being.

Various religions want to fight over whose "god" is the true god/goddess. All of your gods and goddesses are an ASPECT of the Supreme. Some just feel more attracted to certain aspects of the Supreme than others. Some are more attracted to the masculine, some are more attracted to the feminine, some are more attracted to the forgiving aspects of the Supreme and some are more attracted to the vengeful side of the Supreme. Some are more attracted to the dark side, some more attracted to the light and in all of this THOSE ARE ALL ASPECTS OF THE SUPREME. Do you think you know all there is to know about the Supreme? No! Please do not try to place the Supreme in your self-made and/or society-made container. Do you think you can actually love the WHOLE of the Supreme? Anything is possible, but that is an awesome accomplishment. The Supreme is all-encompassing and many do not realize what this means. That is why I seek to understand another person's point of view concerning the Supreme because it will allow me to expand my own perspective. Notice I said, "perspective" because everything we see, hear, experience, etc is altered by our own perceptions, but even our own perceptions are an aspect of the Supreme. Just remember that although they are an aspect of the Supreme, they do **not** make up the WHOLE of the

Supreme. Our perceptions are limited, but that is how we can learn a lot from those who see the world differently than we do. I hope I am clear. Every single thing you see, everything you experience, everything you have been through and every person you have encountered is a part of the Supreme. We are not currently required to love all there is about the Supreme (we have not evolved that far as of yet), ***but we are attracted to and we attract certain aspects of the Supreme for our own life lesson***. The Supreme is way too big to put in our little boxes.

There is no name for the Supreme for the Supreme is not limited yet EVERY name describes the Supreme. That is why I am continuously saying, "Supreme"; I do not know how else to describe such a Force. When a person calls on the Supreme by using a name, they are harnessing the powers of that ASPECT of the Supreme but that does not mean that the Supreme is only limited by that name. There are many names you can call on for specific results. Even within various religions, they have various names for their deity (which is another aspect of the Supreme) depending on the type of energies they are trying to attract for a certain situation.

With all this being said, my question to you is: Who are you? I will tell you who you are. You are an aspect of the Supreme whether "good", "bad", "happy", "sad", "ugly" or "proud", the Supreme is in YOU.

After Thoughts

The meaning of "The Supreme" and how it ties into Increasing Our Vibrations

The above post was written to allow you to consider the idea that every single thing that occurs in this Universe was meant to be no matter how awful or uncomfortable it may be. We tend to separate our good experiences from our bad experiences in order to convince ourselves that there is no place for the "not-so-comfy" realities. Once we see everything as a whole, we will further line up with the ever-evolving vibrations of Mother Earth. The old way was to see things from a duality perspective, but the new way is to see them all as stemming from the same Source with a purpose. This is the perfect time for me to introduce another article. I call it, "Positivity/Negativity'. No matter what you are going through, please know that there is a purpose behind it all. We all have different ways in which we learn and that is why we all have differing experiences. Sometimes when the Supreme is sending us a message and we do not get it the first, second or even third time, these messages will be sent until we GET IT. Nonetheless, the Supreme is patient but also impatient because when the first lesson is not learned, the second one will be even harsher in order to better call your attention to a specific situation or habit that you are ignoring.

Mini-Article VI

Positivity/Negativity

The positives as well as negatives in our lives are both used by the Universe to propel us forward. Sometimes we may feel as though the negatives are setbacks, but they do not have to be! Everything is based on how YOU choose to utilize YOUR experiences to YOUR benefit.

Who are you to only experience positivity? Are YOU only composed of positive traits? No! We mirror the Universe which is a mixture of "good" and "evil", darkness and light, sickness and health, life and death and everything in between.

Some who were born physically disabled have happier more fulfilling lives than those who were born with all their limbs. Why is this? Why do some of those who are termed, "handicapped" smile and experience true joy? Because he/she chooses to and you can too!

What is it that you feel is holding you back? Why do you perceive it to be a setback? Is this supposed setback the end of your life? Is no recovery possible? We must think about things a little deeper than we do.

There are two different types of people I have observed: The first type have been through a lot of stress in their lives and it shows in their mental, emotional, spiritual and physical bodies. The other type I have observed are the ones who have been through a great deal as well (even facing death) yet they appear untouched by life's fury. You see, the difference between those who have a more positive disposition towards life compared to those who focus mostly on their negative experiences have allowed life to get them down. Life's purpose is not to do that; life is meant to teach you lessons that are specific to your life purpose, to make you stronger and wiser, and lastly, to give you an opportunity to evolve. The people who focus more on their positive experiences and learn from the negative ones know how to mold the negativity to their advantage. They OWN their own lives. They take an unfavorable experience and say, "I will use you to my advantage!" They do not really say this aloud, but I am sure they are subconsciously saying it.

Life is full of positivity and negativity but how do YOU plan on using your experiences to propel yourself forward?

I would also like to add that sometimes life continuously throws the same negative experiences to us because we give out the signal that we enjoy them. Patience is NOT always a good thing. When you allow yourself to be patient with a particular circumstance, it will rare its ugly head continuously until you let the Universe know through thought, word and action that those experiences will stop and that there is no more room for them. Take charge!

It is all in YOUR hands!

After Thoughts

The meaning of "Positivity/Negativity" and How it Ties into Increasing Our Vibrations

The above post was written to express that negative experiences do not automatically knock us out of the game. We can roll with the punches of life! Knowing how to roll with the punches and also knowing how to punch back will help you to increase your vibrations because you are fully engaged in your own life. Appreciate the positives that you experience and learn from the negatives. You must also know when enough to enough. Do not let challenges and issues get you down!

Brief Overview

* Accept and understand your lower self and also your higher self (both are necessary in evolution).
* The Kingdom of Heaven is inside of you (within your crown chakra)!
* Do not jump the gun! Crawl before you walk.
* Understand YOUR connection to the earth, her inhabitants and to the Universe itself.
* Understand the need for everything that exists whether pleasant or unpleasant. Know that YOU are an aspect of the Supreme so you are very much needed.

* Know that duality is what is allowing us and the Universe to grow together, but the veils are coming down.
* Release illogical fears. Life is not meant to get you down, but to allow you to grow!
* Take charge of your own life!

These are Practical Methods You can Use to Increase YOUR Vibrations TODAY!

Clearing Your Thoughts for a New Beginning (Getting Rid of Emotional Fogs)

You will need:
- White candle
- Sandalwood incense sticks
- Natural Sea Salt
- White Bowl of water

Prepare a white bowl of water that you will pour a little salt into. Salt helps to absorb negativity. The bowl should be white because it will help to clear your thoughts.

Light the candle and burn the incense.

Place the white bowl that has the water/salt mixture on top of your head as you meditate.

Think with the intentions of allowing your thoughts to become clearer and clearer. Allow the bowl of salt water to absorb any leftover negative thoughts and allow the color white to clear your mind. (Do this until you feel you should stop).

After you have cleared your mind, put the bowl down and let your mind wonder. Just relax. Do not focus your thoughts. Let them flow like the water.
Flush the water that was in the bowl down the toilet. Wash your hands. Rinse the bowl out and add water with a little salt again but this time put your hands in the bowl and sprinkle the water around your body. This helps to cleanse your aura.
End this ritual whenever you like.

Connecting with Mother Earth

Eat more natural foods straight from mother earth and less store-bought foods. Go to your local farmer's market or a place that sells organic foods. If you can grow a garden in your own backyard, that would be even better! When chemicals, human hands and technology are used to handle our foods, those interferences keep us out of touch with the earth and her vibrations. Reduce the intake of processed foods and pharmaceutical drugs.

Lotus Chakra H ealing™

This is an overview of where the 7 chakras are, what colors they carry and what they govern. I will also show you how to use the symbol of the lotus to help cleanse your chakras and also to increase your vibrations within 30 minutes or less!

Chakra	Location	Governs
Root / Red	Base of spine by coccyx	Survival
Sacral / Orange	Between navel and pelvic bone	Joy
Solar Plexus/ Yellow	Between navel and sternum	Power
Heart / Green	Middle of chest	Love/Relationships
Throat / Blue	In front of thyroid	Communication
3rd Eye / Violet	Between eyebrows	Intuition
Crown / White	Top of head	Spiritual Connection

Now that you understand the chakras a little better if you have not already, you can perform this meditation.

Imagine your chakras as balls of rotating lights in the color that is designated to them in the chart in the location that they reside on your body. Imagine that all of them are spinning and are shining bright lights. Now picture a lotus growing from underneath murky water and out into the light of day! The murky soil they reside in is under water and that is where the root chakra is. Allow it to grow up towards your sacral chakra and then your solar plexus. As it reaches your heart chakra, you begin to see the top of the lotus break through the surface of the water. Allow it to grow and grow until it reaches the crown chakra.

Increasing your vibrations is likened unto a lotus that grows in murky waters and rises to meet the beautiful rays of the sun.

Be like the beautiful lotus that you know is within you and shine bright to the world. Shine your light!

Protecting Your Energies (Especially for Counselors)
You will need:
- Gardenias

Just carry gardenias with you in your purse or in your pocket as a way to help bring more protection. This will help you to arm yourself with more protection using the protective energies of gardenia. This is great to carry while you are counseling another person.

Protection and Releasing Fear

You will need:
- Activated Charcoal (powder form) - can be found at local health food store
- Black bowl
- Black Candle
- Water

Place water and mix it with activated charcoal inside of a bowl. Place this bowl on top of your head and think of all those thoughts that cause you fear and allow the charcoal to absorb them for you. You can do this while burning a black candle (black candles symbolize protection). (Do this for however long you feel is right).

Flush the bowl of water down toilet when finished to symbolize flushing down your fears.
After this, just allow yourself to meditate and get inside of your own thoughts by allowing them to wonder.

Sharpening Your 3rd Eye (Diet)
You will need:
- Pineapples/Tropical Fruits (or fruits in general)
- Vegetables
The 3rd eye is connected to the pineal gland and this gland is stimulated by fruits and vegetables.
Increase your fruit and vegetable intake while also increasing how much water you drink. ***A cleansed body is a cleansed spirit.***

Sharpening Your 3rd Eye (Sandalwood)
You will need:
- Sandalwood oil
- Sandalwood Incense

Place a small dab of sandalwood oil slightly above your eyelids and/or on your temples.
Burn the sandalwood incense and then meditate to your favorite relaxation music or without music. Just make

sure the environment is suitable to relaxation.

Sharpening Your 3rd Eye (Sun Gazing/Flame Gazing)
You will need:
- Sun
- Indigo-colored Candle

Be very careful when gazing at the sun because there is a specific art to it. When I sun gaze, I do it from the inside of my room and I peek out the window to such a degree that the curtains block the intense rays and I can actually see the circular-shape of the sun. You can gaze between 5-10 minutes every day.

If you are concerned about sun gazing, you can try getting an Indigo-colored candle and gaze at it between 5-10 minutes every day.

If you want to really supercharge your 3rd eye, sun gaze during the day and flame gaze at night. You can do this along with eating more fruits and vegetables and also referring back to the sandalwood oil and incense ritual.

Sharpening Your 3rd Eye While Sleeping
You will need:
- Hematite

In order to sharpen intuition while sleeping, place hematite stone either under your pillow or in your head scarf(*if you wear one at night*). It will give you dreams that tell what will happen in the future or it can give you more insight into a certain situation.

Last Thoughts:

How Does Increasing Our Vibrations Relate to Goddess Energies?

I know you may be wondering why I have brought you all this way without telling you how this all relates to the Goddess. How does this all tie in with the Goddess? Well the earth is a living, breathing, FEELING entity and is considered, by some, to be a GODDESS that supplies our needs. Many of us have been very ungrateful for the sacrifices made by her. Never forget your Mother! We will not evolve if we cannot properly evolve with the earth. The same way we honor our earthly mothers who gave us life, fed us and kept us alive, we must also honor Mother Earth. THAT is how we will evolve thereby, INCREASING our vibrations with the earth's vibrations and this article has given you the tools so that you can do just that.

The Cold, Hard Truth

Know this because this is IMPORTANT for all to know. Without this knowledge, people will continue to travel backward in evolution rather than forward and unnecessary suffering will surely continue: **Life starts in the Womb. This Universe is One Great Big WOMB. The Feminine Principle of Creation has** been denied, and as a result, women deny themselves of WHO and WHAT they are. KNOW WHO YOU ARE. There is absolutely nothing that can be created without the feminine. Observe nature. How things work in the spiritual realm is manifested in the physical realm. KNOW the truth of how nature and the supernatural realm work. The Goddess knows how to build, but also knows how to destroy. Let this be known, SHE will progress forward with or without you! Know where you came from; know the ROOT of all things and that is the womb. You came from one so it would be foolish to deny yourself of your origins. If the Womb is not happy/healthy, all that is birthed from the womb will be sick.

A New Tomorrow

I truly believe a new tomorrow will come, but we have to do our parts. There are a lot of earth changes and shifts in the atmosphere that are occurring around us right now, but do not fear; it gets worse before it gets better and Mother Earth is now in the process of moving into the 5th dimension. In the 3rd dimension, materialism wins out, but in the 5th dimension, it is more about Spirit, love and acceptance. The veils are coming down. We will learn why there is light and darkness, why there is sickness and health, why there is "good" and "bad". Remember, it is ALL Supreme; those elements exist with a purpose even if

77

we may not presently understand why. All of these elements are within us. I hope you took from this book a different perspective on your view of life. What I have spoken about is not written in stone and I would not claim it to be, but even what I took the time to write to you is also a part of the Supreme. May this message benefit your personal evolutionary journey! Thanks so much for taking the time to engage in reading this article.

Do as You are Led

In closing, I would like to encourage you to create on your own rituals if you are led to do so. Please create from your heart, spirit and mind. *From this day forward, after reading through this article and also using its practical applications, you should begin to observe a noticeable change in your life and in the lives of others.* When we allow ourselves to evolve, everything else around us evolves too. Whether other people have to leave your life because your vibrations are too intense for them or you attract those who are vibrating at your level, you will be on your way to increasing your vibrations with Mother Earth! Your personal new day is here!

4 The Sacred Source

By Tonya K. Freeman D.D MsD

Too many women have sex simply because. The reasons are many. They don't want to feel left out. They feel that sex with anyone is better than sex with no one. They do it out of revenge for having been raped or molested. They just don't know any better. They don't realize that the womb is the Sacred Source of life. They are not aware of the most precious gift of creativity. Sexual energy…and what a powerful energy it is.

The Sacred Source is called Yoni in India. The translation of the Yoni in Sanskrit is womb, origin, source or vulva. According to Rufus Camphausen in his book, Yoni: Creative Symbol of Feminine Power, the word Yoni is broken down in this manner…Y = the animating principle, the heart, the true self, union, O = preservation, brightness I = love, desire, consciousness, to shine, to pervade, pain, sorrow, N = lotus, Motherhood, menstrual cycle, nakedness, emptiness, pearl.

The I and the N change position. Though it is spelled Yoin it is pronounced yonee.

In many cultures the Yoni is considered to be magical. It has a very powerful magnetic force. It has the ability to heal and to protect. In Ancient Egypt, Africa, India, Greece and the Pacific Islands, there was a deeper insight into the power of the Yoni. This energy of dispelling evil forces, averting disasters or even banishing unwanted guests originates in the woman through proper use of Yonic energy.

Yoni drawings were displayed on buildings to keep evil at bay and you can still find some of these carved figures known as Sheela Na Gig in present day Ireland, England, Scotland, France and Germany.

Those who possess a degree of esoteric knowledge recognize the geometric symbol that represents the Yoni is an inverted or downward pointing triangle. In alchemy as in astrology this triangle is used to represent the elements of earth and water, both of which are the feminine principle. There are those who send prayers through an inverted triangle. It is said to carry much power by those who use it often.

All too often women do not understand how precious they really are. If they did, there would not be the insecurities that many are faced with about their sexual self. I am not passing judgment but making an observation based on what I have seen and heard over the years, as well as having experienced for myself firsthand what the lack of knowledge and appreciation of oneself can do to the psyche and the body for that matter.

Many women become Mothers and because they are not taught properly about sexual energy, they cannot teach their children and a vicious cycle reigns supreme. There are many books that speak to Sacred Sexuality, Tantra, the Tao of Sex and the Secrets of Sex. Most of these books are excellent sources of information. Workshops are being held all over the United States regarding this very subject matter. Some of these workshops if not most are completely above board and teach couples how to enjoy one another, how to contain the sexual energy that it may be used to heal the body, but some are just out for meeting people and swapping partners. I do not condemn nor condone such a practice. I am more in line with having one very special partner that you love and can express the joyful, powerful and pleasurable energy with.

There are breathing techniques that one can learn to help redirect the sexual energy throughout the entire body. In this way, the energy is used for helpful, healing purposes rather than harmful purposes.

Of course there is so much more that can be written about this subject. I merely wanted to peak your interest and your curiosity that you may do some research on your own.

When women remember and reclaim the beauty and the sacredness of their very existence, it will add to the healing of a world out of sync.

5 Energy and the Ra Sekhi Energy Healing System

by Nia Yaa Nebhet

My first significant lesson about energy came when I was 13 years old. I went to see a horror movie. I was not a fearful person but the effects of watching that movie stayed with me for weeks after. I had nightmares and was terrified of the killer being under my bed or in my closet. My cousin, who had gone with me to the movie, laughed during the movie and laughed at me for being so scary. I realized there was something about me that made the movie more real to me. I decided then that I would not watch anymore horror movies because I did not like the feelings or the fear, that came with seeing someone murder people over and over. I still don't watch horror movies because I realized that my energy is very sensitive to negative energy and I don't like things that upset me, things that are evil, or crazy. That is not the kind of energy for me. It interrupts my natural peace. As my journey continued I began to learn more about energy, about healing, working with nature and the connection between these things.

Energy is the unseen force that is in all living things. Energy cannot be created or destroyed, it just is. Energy is in the sun, moon, stars, the Earth, water and everything living. It flows around and within us. It vibrates through colors, sound, symbols and all things living. As humans, it surrounds us and moves through us via our blood and our breath. Our energy moves through us in patterns of vibration, also called energy fields, in the same way that a song moves through patterns of energetic vibrations. So therefore if our energy vibration is high, the energy we consume is high, the energy we attract, what we think and speak has a high vibration as well. Our energy is primarily fed through our thoughts, what we consume and our environment. However all things that affect our senses also affect our energy and our vibration.

Our personal energy is called our life force. It is connected to our breath, blood and our spirit and leaves our body when we make our transition. It continues to be a part of the all, the universal energy that sustains us all. Our life force energy is called sekhem, prana, chi or ki. Most of us are unaware of this energy and therefore don't ever reach our greatest potential. Those who become aware of it and learn to control it can do things such as break a stack of bricks, overcome any obstacles, astral travel, manifest things, etc.... There are many techniques available for cultivating sekhem. Meditating, doing yoga, tai chi, chi gong or other martial arts share valuable lessons on developing and building sekhem/chi.

Our sekhem is connected to our will, our drive to live and our motivation to get things done. So when our energy is high we have the ability to do what we need to do in a timely fashion. When we are behind in our work or find ourselves procrastinating it is associated with low vitality and is associated with how we feel, how we are thinking, etc....We have to consciously do things to keep our sekhem balanced, strong and with a high vibration. Remember that everything that affects your senses affects your energy, your sekhem. Things that you see, hear, smell, taste, touch and feel can bring your vibration up or down. This is why we eat sweets though we know it is not good for our bodies; it is sweet and good for our spirit. It can make you feel good and raise your energy because it tastes good, have it now and then as a treat, because overall too much chocolate can cause problems in your physical body which will lower your vibration.

When we go through good experiences it is good for our energy, it raises our vibration. When we go through traumatic experiences it creates negative vibrations, our energy level decreases and our energy field changes. If we go through several traumatic experiences, our energy field can build layers of unbalanced energy. For example black women who have gone through lifetimes of traumatic experiences create children who are born with layers of negative energy fields. So we come back to the Earth with energy that was not healed and processed in previous lifetimes which can lead to negative behavior patterns, poor character, negative thinking habits, and so on.

We come here at this time with the opportunity to bring these things, our energy (inner chi) into balance. We have a chance to correct our mistakes, learn our lessons , raise our vibrations and experience the ascension of our souls. We come to correct ourselves and make ourselves more perfect, or Christ like. It is up to every individual to find their mission in life, their purpose and to fulfill it to the best of their ability. It is also up to everyone to see their shortcomings, to learn their lessons and to live in MAAT, or with good character. That is the God force, the Goddess within us that we all come here with. We are made in the image and likeness of the Goddess and that gives us the power and energy to manifest all things. When we are aware that our energy is universal and infinite we know we are connected to the all. Our abilities and possibilities become unlimited.

Our connection to the infinite source gives us the ability to create our lives the way that we want and live our dreams because that is in alignment with our highest self. It gives us the ability to heal ourselves and to do everything that we desire to have all that we desire all that we need and more. Our thoughts, words, actions and energy create our world. When you understand energy, how to protect and keep your energy high, you can create a better world for yourself. See yourself as a part of the energy flow, a being which absorbs and releases energy constantly. You can choose to take and radiate high or low frequency energy. The high frequency energy includes love, harmony, peace, joy and positive feeling, the lower the frequency the lower the feelings disappointment, doubt; sadness, anger and fear are the lowest. You can tell where your energy is based on high you feel. You can also control or choose how you are going to feel.

The mind controls the way you think and the way you feel. its knowledge or level of consciousness, the ego, thinking patterns, behavior, intentions, imagination, dreams, focus also effect the energy and the sekhem as well as the ability to use sekhem. When the mind, the heart and the will are in agreement then one is balanced and in MAAT. The fruits of being on this energetic vibration are success, joy, physical or financial gains and most importantly peace within. These are people who seem to have it all, not the rich and famous but the ones who have successful businesses or nonprofits; they have beautiful families and seem to be happy and healthy no matter what happens. That is the peace and happiness we all seek to have, heaven on earth.

We have energy that flows within us. As women, it comes up from the earth through our feet and move up through our back to our head and then moves down to our feet and back up again. For men it comes from the heavens through the crown, moves down and back around. You will find that as we get older many of us begin to have problems in our knees and hips, because the energy becomes blocked at these points from us sitting upright in chairs for so many days. That is why it is so important to exercise, to keep the air, the blood and energy flowing through us properly. Any form of dance, all sports, walking, swimming are all excellent ways to keep your energy flowing, your life force strong and keep you healthy overall.

We have energy that flows around us as a protective force field. Some call it an aura. The aura is supposed to keep you away from things and people that are not good for you as well as keep them away from you. It should keep people from absorbing or using your energy in a negative way. Our auras are also affected by our inner chi, our life force and chakras. When they are strong they protect us and radiate bright colors. However they can be torn, ripped, grey, weak or otherwise damaged and may not work the way they are meant to. Sometimes others energy can become attached to our aura as well. The aura is strong when you have good character, are living in alignment, eating well, exercising, getting proper rest, being loved, balanced home life etc....The aura is made of electromagnetic energy and will attract what it is. That is like the law of attraction, what you think and feel is your energy and that is what you attract whether positive or negative. You can use spiritual baths, crystals, incense, oils, or other natural tools to clear and reinforce your aura.

We have concentrated areas of energy within us called chakras. They swirl in a circular motion very quickly and are seen as small wheels within us. Their speed depends on one's vitality; if ones energy is high they move very quickly. If one has a low vibration they move slowly and sometimes not at all. There are 7 major chakra located along our spine, 22 minor chakras throughout our bodies, one chakra below our feet which connects us to the earth and at least 3 chakras over our head which connects us to the heavens. The chakras give, receive and store energy. It is at these points where energy comes into us and from these points vital energy is sent to our organs, glands and other parts of our body. This energy is what keeps everything working as it should. So if our life force is low on energy there is not much to be used and dis-ease begins in the physical. Every physical ailment comes from a spiritual, mental or emotional issue that has not been process properly, therefore it causes a block in energy flow and creates sickness in the body to get you to pay attention and address your issues. Remember energy can attach itself to you, your thoughts, feelings and/or your aura. You may feel a shift in energy when you aritu or chakras are out of balance. Sometimes you feel a shift in energy and are unaware of what you are really feeling. We will discuss some ways to balance and raise your energy.

In working to keep your vibration high you want to be mindful of the things that you consume because they also affect the energy. Not just the things that you eat but also the things you see, listen to and the people you are around. When you eat foods that are alive, foods that are raw and organic, if possible, you will receive the highest amount of energy from them. When you drink fresh carrot juice you feel it instantly rejuvenating your body as it flows through your system. Not only because it is liquid and gets in your blood faster, but also fresh juice is still living so it has more vitality, vitamins, minerals and energy then cooked foods. It is said that eating food that is still attached to the ground is the best way to eat because the food is still fully charged with energy. Foods that are cooked lose their vitamin, mineral and energy levels. So as you see your veggies turning from a bright green to a dull green color it is losing its energy or vitality. So it cannot add very much to your own energy. Packaged, processed and junk food does not add to your energy, in fact they may lower your energy because they introduce foreign, man-made chemicals into your body. Remember your life force does flow through your blood which also feeds your heart and brain. So things you take in will affect your energy.

Be mindful of the things you watch, what you read and look at throughout your day. Watching violent or dramatic images will lower your energetic vibration.

Most TV programs, advertising, magazines and newspapers work to over stimulate our lower energy. They keep us sad, angry or upset which keeps us from being balanced overall. I have found the same to be true with the music available to us today. When we hear words spoken to us repeatedly every day, it becomes like a chant and begins to influence our psyche and energy fields. Just at the TV and radio works on electric waves for us to see and hear it, those same electric wave patterns affect our own patterns.

There are several healing modalities and natural tools that you can use to balance, clear and enhance your energy fields. Some of my favorite ones are listed below.

1.   Sound therapy- using crystal bowls, tuning forks, bells, rattles, music, chanting, etc…

2.   Aromatherapy – using essential oils and incense

3.   Color therapy – using material, candles, colored light bulbs, colored paper, etc…

4.   Touch therapy – using acupressure or massage

5.   Fasting – clearing your body of toxins and waste

6.   Crystal therapy – using crystals, wearing crystals, crystal grids, crystal elixirs

These tools and more are used in the Ra Sekhi Energy Healing System.

Ra Sekhi Energy Healing System

    Ra Sekhi is an energy healing system that is modeled on the ancient principles of Ancient Kemetic Healing. It is a holistic way to bring about healing in the mind, body, emotions, and spirit. The initiation process reprograms and reconnects one with the ancestral healing rites. I first came to know of healing with energy through Reiki, a Japanese form of energy healing. Over the years, I came to know of the Goddess Sekhmet who is known for healing. She came to me through the process of my own personal healing work. Through her connection, I came to realize the origins of the Reiki practice was through our ancestors of ancient Kemet.

Sekhmet directed and charged me with teaching our people to work with energy. She explained that this system could help to heal our people and our communities as well as be able to see the positive changes that we want to see in our lives. As we call on her more, we will be able to break destructive cycles. She is known to restore Maat when there is chaos. That may be toxins within our body, negative habits, and toxic environments. A lot of our energy is often blocked and it is through energy that blocked energy patterns are broken and we are able to use our personal power to achieve our dreams. As one person becomes a light in each city, then two, and three and the light gets brighter and brighter raising our vibration and ascending our souls. So, ultimately, as we heal, we heal others, and heal the world.

The Meaning of Ra Sekhi

Ra Sekhi was born out of my Sekhmet connection. Ra is from Ra or Raat which is not the sun, but the energy that we feel from the sun. Sekhem is our personal life force. Shekem is within her name and is her energy. Ra Sekhi is the connection between the solar energy and our personal life force.

Core Principles of Ra Sekhi

The core principles of Ra Sekhi are in alignment with Maat. This means that they have to cultivate pure minds, pure bodies, and pure hearts in order to be able to channel the energy to heal in the way it was meant to be. While we are all human, we encourage others to be the best that we can be. To that end, our process involves purification and also in developing a strong mental power using the mind, focus, concentration, visualization. It also teaches to release the mind to the spiritual realm so that the energy can flow.

Our great ancestors lived by the 42 laws of the Goddess Maat. These Laws of MAAT are also known as the Declaration of Innocence. They are drawn from the "Pert Em HRU" (the Book of Coming Forth By Day) the oldest Afrikan book of holy scriptures. With these laws, our Ancient Ancestors maintained a society without policemen for thousands of years. These are affirmative statements that declared how we will live our lives and form the foundation for ethical living. There are several translations of these declarations. Here is one:

42 Laws of Maat

1. I honor virtue
2. I benefit with gratitude
3. I am peaceful
4. I respect the property of others
5. I affirm that all life is sacred
6. I give offerings that are genuine
7. I live in truth
8. I regard all altars with respect
9. I speak with sincerity
10. I consume only my fair share
11. I offer words of good intent
12. I relate in peace
13. I honor animals with reverence
14. I can be trusted
15. I care for the earth
16. I keep my own council
17. I speak positively of others
18. I remain in balance with my emotions
19. I am trustful in my relationships
20. I hold purity in high esteem
21. I spread joy
22. I do the best I can
23. I communicate with compassion
24. I listen to opposing opinions
25. I create harmony
26. I invoke laughter
27. I am open to love in various forms
28. I am forgiving

29. I am kind
30. I act respectfully of others
31. I am accepting
32. I follow my inner guidance
33. I converse with awareness
34. I do good
35. I give blessings
36. I keep the waters pure
37. I speak with good intent
38. I praise the Goddess and the God
39. I am humble
40. I achieve with integrity
41. I advance through my own abilities
42. I embrace the All

Techniques for Ra Sekhi Healing

We use palm healing techniques to heal. We also use Kemetic and other African symbols. Some symbols are commonly known and some less common. They are used to bring about changes on energetic levels. Interestingly, some of the symbols in my level one are used in other systems that people pay thousands of dollars for. We also use Kemetic mantras and the power of sound in our voices. We also use African instruments in our sound healing. Color therapy in the form of candles, but also as visualization is incorporated and materials. We use other natural tools from east, west, and south African traditions. We use these things to impact the aura and to bring about Maat or Balance in our selves, families, clients, and community.

The 5 Levels of Initiation in Ra Sekhi

Level 1 focuses on self-healing. It is the beginning of the initiates path as a healer. This level helps to cultivate Sekhem (inner-chi) and develop spiritual- mental connection. It also promotes realignment and harmony of the emotional, mental, physical and spiritual bodies. Initiates open a connection with Spirit Guides, balance the chakras, and clears the aura. They learn core principles about living in MAAT and more. This level also includes and attunement (blessing from teacher),healing session, breathing technique, palm healing, daily precepts, symbols, chakras, color therapy and more. This level is often taught online.

Level 2 is the practitioner level. Those that can master energy for themselves, can then begin to work on others. Initiates here are certified as a practitioner. This level strengthens healer's knowledge and connection with Sekhem, also allows the healer to generate more energy and concentration. It enhances spiritual connection, builds Ashe (spiritual energy), practitioners develop intuition and learn how to use a pendulum, sound therapy, and higher level of concentration and more. Distance healing, symbols , crystals, mantras, pendulums, chakra balancing, aura cleansing, spiritual protection are also a part of this level. This and the levels to follow must be taught in person.

Level 3 is a 2 part Master teacher level. It takes a minimum of a year to complete because of the nature of the work of moving from practitioner to a teacher. Only those who have a sincere calling will reach this level. This level requires a series of elemental (air, fire, water, earth) purification rituals. Purification rites on the summer solstice weekend is a part of this rite as well as a 21 day fast. '

Level 4 is Priesthood level where the teacher becomes a Priest or Priestess and is initiated into the priesthood of Sehkmet. Strict requirements are demanded to be fulfilled at this level.

Level 5 Rakeet level is the known as the keeper of knowledge and the mysteries. As of this writing, I am the only one who is at this level.

Tools used in RaSekhi

Healing Wands are used to channel energy for healing. They are used to manifest things, protect, heal, clear aura, activate the chakras.

Pendulums read and program energy. We work with them to remove blockages, activate the chakras, detect issues that one may not be aware of.

Spiritual Baths are important in removing the layers that we have around us and in us. They help us with unseen energy. They help clear things and help extract things and used for protections.

Crystals

Crystals are powerful tools that I use often in my energy work. They have been used since ancient times, all over the world. They magnify the energy of the one wearing them as well as the environment they are in. The electromagnetic vibrations of each crystal are based on the minerals they are made of. They are very helpful in clearing the aura, balancing the chakras, balancing emotions, enhancing spiritual connection, protection against negative energy, astral travel, meditation and many more things. They are formed over hundreds or thousands of years so they also carry memory of past times. When working with crystals it is best to touch them or allow them to touch your skin. When you perspire while holding a crystal you are able to absorb the energy from the crystal even more. They are said to have healing qualities for the mind, body and spirit. Even if you wear a crystal and it doesn't touch your skin, you can still feel the benefits of its energy. They are also said to be even more powerful for melaninated ones, our melanin allows us to absorb and use the energy of crystals on a higher level than others.

Quartz is one of my favorite crystals. It is one that everyone should have at least one of. Clear quartz is known to radiate positive energy, it helps keep you clear, and it balances and activates the chakras. It is healing, activating, can raise your vibration and enhance your spiritual powers. It can be worn every day or in the home or office. It can transmute negative energy, so it should be cleaned often. There are many varieties of clear quartz, elestial quartz helps one connect with their highest self. Lemurian and Tibetan quartz are other varieties worth checking into, they are both said to be highly spiritual, highly charged and very powerful.

Another powerful and popular stone is amethyst. It can range from a deep purple to a light violet color and even clear or white. The color of the stone helps one determine the vibration of the stone. The stronger or darker the color the shorter the waves are so it moves quicker and feels stronger than more pastel like shade. Amethyst is known as an all heal crystal. It works with all chakras, but especially the crown. It can enhance ones spiritual connection and powers, so it is good to hold while praying or meditating. Sleeping with amethyst will enhance your dream state and wearing amethyst will protect you from negative influences and drama.

Citrine is another excellent stone to work with and to have around. It works to activate and stimulate your life force energy. It can clear your aura, your thoughts and emotions. It also transmutes negative energy. It is good to transmute negative effects of radioactive energy. Citrine is a powerful addition to crystal grids and can be used to clean energy from other crystals. Because many crystals absorb energy it is important to clean them often, like once a month or every season if you work with them often. You can use natural things to clean crystals like sunlight, moonlight, seawater or rainwater, salt, lemon or berry juice can be used as well. I also like to bury mine in the earth and let them sit for 3 to 7 or more days, I do this once a year at least because I work with my crystals so much. I have found that hard crystals like quartz can be clean with almost everything. Softer crystals like malachite, angelite, jade, infinite, selenite, etc....do not like to be cleaned with salt water, it will alter the color and energy of your stone.

Black stones are important to have because they are the most powerful stones for absorbing negative energy, protecting against psychic attack and they are very grounding. You can choose between black tourmaline which also protects against radiation, obsidian, jet or black jasper. Be careful with hematite which will sometimes break after absorbing negative energy or it may irritate your energy field and give you headaches (in some cases). Black stones are good to wear or keep in your home or office, to keep positive energy flowing in your environment.

When I became aware of how crystals work, I placed them all around my home. I begin to notice that when people came to my house they would always say the home was peaceful, calming and welcoming. People seemed so glad to come and did not want to leave because the energy in the house was so positive. I attribute the peaceful vibe to the crystals and aromatherapy that I was doing at the time.

Lapis lazuli is another good stone that has been used since ancient times. It can work to enhance your intuition and your ability to see clearly. It is soothing to the mental and emotions. It stimulates spiritual powers, protects against psychic attack, promotes harmony and stimulates your mind. You can place it on your first eye or throat chakra while meditating. Ask to see and speak more clearly or affirm that your psychic powers are strong. This is another good stone to sleep with to enhance your dream work.

Rose quartz is very good for working with the heart and issues of heart. It radiates unconditional love, self-love, harmony and peace. It is good to work with to balance and heal the heart and relationships. Many Sisters develop breast cancer because of heart/relationship issues that have not been processed properly. The heart becomes hard because of bitterness, sadness or anger; these emotions can lead to the development of tumors. Using crystals and other natural things to process that energy, thoughts and emotions can prevent those kinds of diseases. You can use rose quartz by holding it in your hand or putting it directly on your heart. Say affirmations of love, healing and forgiveness. Release negative thoughts and emotions and do this whenever you are feeling sad or angry to help change your vibration quickly.

There are other purple stones that are very good to work with charoite, sugalite and lepidolite. They all work with the crown chakra, they enhance your spiritual connection, promote self -love and assist you with connecting to your higher self. There is another purple stone from South Africa called the spiritual mystic quartz. It is made with amethyst, citrine and quartz and is super powerful. The colors vary but it is recognized by the crystalized patterns that surround the stone. It looks like hundreds of tiny crystals together to form a larger crystal, so each one is made of tiny universes that are connected. This stone is said to be very good to heal divisions within self, in families and communities. I use it often in my healing sessions as well as when I'm doing work with groups. When I saw this stone for the first time my spirit told me that it was important for our people and our families to have some of these powerful crystals.

You can also program your crystals to work with you the way you need them too. After you clean them and hold them and talk into them. Share your needs and speak your intentions into them, asking them to work with you and share their healing medicine with you. After working with crystals for some time you can also learn to make crystal grids, elixirs and other uses for them as well.

As melaninated people working with energy is innate, because our ancestors were so deeply connected to nature and lived with a higher consciousness. They mastered their energy and were able to project themselves, speak without words, move things with their minds, communicate with all of nature, etc....The Ra Sekhi healing system helps us to reconnect with this mastery. It is our right and our heritage to live in MAAT, with righteousness and balanced, positive energy. It is our duty to return to our natural Divine selves and restore MAAT within our lives and those with whom we are connected. I give thanks for this Divine Time and the Beautiful World which we are creating as we return to our Greatness and the Restoration of the Goddess on Earth. THE POWER IS IN OUR HANDS!!!!!!!!!!!!!!!!

6 The Journey Within: Tapping into Your Personal Power through Sacred Circles

By Shante "LIFE" Duncan

There I stood, a beautiful wombman with so much "potential", yet I couldn't seem to rid myself of the negativity that plagued my mind and thoughts. A part of me acknowledged the power I possess, yet the other part of me felt vulnerable and dissatisfied.

Throughout my life, I was withered with insecurities, but it was not until I cried out to the Universe asking to be the person God created me to be, that I discovered my Goddess. The Ancestors heard my cries and immediately birthed within me S.H.E.R.A.H. (Sisters Helping Each Other Reach A Higher Height), a women's movement that changed my life and reactivated my Goddess. I journeyed within myself and discovered a very precious and sacred part of me.

I came together with beautiful Goddesses, who were all, representations of me. We all shared so much. We embraced so many dreams, hopes, desires, fears and abilities. We opened our hearts and we began building. We prayed, we meditated, we cried, we healed, we hoped, and we did. We began taking instrumental steps in the process of re-learning and truly loving and honoring ourselves.

We are still on that journey and I am thankful for every lesson learned and every moment shared.
Gathering with other Goddesses on your personal journey is essential. Since ancient times women have gathered to embrace, support and direct each other. They danced under the moon together, they performed rituals together, they sang, they drummed, they gave birth and they bleed all in the name of wombmanhood, divine sisterhood, and peace.

We have come too far in our journey to stop now. If you are not a part of a sister community, then join one. If one does not exist in your area, create one because nothing happens unless something moves! Let's Move!

Starting your Sister/Goddess Circle

1. Identify the purpose

When starting your circle, it is very imperative that you are clear on what the purpose of the circle is and what results you desire for the gathering. There are many different types of sister circles, so be very specific on who you want to attract and what your purpose will be. During this process you should take the time to name the group as well.

2. Plan your gatherings

When planning your gathering, be as specific as possible here as well. What is your agenda? What are your topics? How will the gathering flow? Do you want food or no? If so, what types of food? (At the S.H.E.R.A.H. gatherings we restrict our food to vegetarian/vegan dishes.) Are children allowed? Should the women were specific colors? How active will the other members be? What outcomes do you anticipate? Should it be outside or inside (this will depend on the types of rituals and ceremonies performed)? How long should the gathering be?

3. Promote the gathering

Depending on your target audience, you may choose to use word of mouth or promote it in a community paper, or via any number of social media sites. The key is to ensure through your promotions the nature of your gatherings are well articulated and that you are promoting further enough in advance to ensure your targeted audience can plan to attend.

4. Anticipate a successful gathering

Sometimes when we take on the charge of leading initiatives like forming a sister circle, we become concerned with who's coming and how many people will show up. The reality of it is that whoever is supposed to be there, will be there. Keep your energy clear and stick to your agenda as a way to ensure a successful gathering.

Tapping into Your Personal Power

Although sister circles are essential to our well-being, there are certain things that we need to do to ensure we are keeping our Goddess active. Below, I have outlined 10 things necessary to tapping into your personal power.

1.   PRAYER AND MEDITATION

Because it is important to seek the Most High, prayer is the first and most essential step. You must take the time to communicate with your Higher Power. Offer gratitude and love for your life and seek guidance.

Go into a focused meditation to hear what the Most High and the Ancestors have for you. Seek quiet to learn of the plan and get the directions.

2. *EAT TO LIVE*

What we eat plays a major role in the way that we feel about ourselves. We should eat the appropriate amounts of fruits, vegetables and drink plenty of water. We should eat foods that will give us energy. What we eat is very important to how we behave, I'm sure you have heard the saying, "You are what you eat."
What you eat will dictate the way you live or if you will live.

3. *MOVE YOUR BODY*

A great way to show love to your body is to move it. Exercising is a very progressive and fulfilling activity that contributes positively to your health. It aids your mental and physical state. There are plenty of different ways to workout. You can walk, run or dance, the point is to move with intention. Move to allow your body the chance to properly release unneeded energy and to release all unwanted energy. Embrace Egyptian Yoga and other activities that will keep you moving, stretching and connected to your body. Once you begin to exercise on a regular basis you will notice the change in your attitude. You become more fulfilled because you've released a lot of negative energy when you workout. So, take some time to exercise, however you do it, just do it.

4.HONESTLY COMMUNICATE WITH YOURSELF

We have all been taught the importance of communication. We've been told that communication opens the door to limitless possibilities, so just imagine what we could gain if we were to communicate with ourselves. If we took the time to talk to ourselves and be honest with ourselves, we would appreciate ourselves that much more and we wouldn't look to others for our happiness. We give others so much control of our lives because we feel that they would steer us in some sort of direction. They do, but how often do they take us where we really want to go. Not often. We too often end up living an existence so far from the one we deserve and desire. We then become confused and that's when the war begins. We become impatient with our current realities because we see so clearly what our lives could be like, but we were too afraid to believe in ourselves because we trusted someone else who completely took us off of our paths. If we just learn to be honest with ourselves and be true to ourselves, we would experience an increased amount of inner peace. Follow your dreams and be proud of who you are, even if you are not at that ultimate stage that you seek, take pride in knowing that you can get there.

5. PERFORM DAILY SELF-AFFIRMATIONS

It's very important to believe in yourself. Throughout the scriptures of (Jesus), he spoke on himself and yet he never spoke a negative word regarding his self. We tend to doubt ourselves and we say what we can't do and what we don't have and we focus on what we don't look like. Jesus said, "I Am that I Am."

With that being said, look yourself in the mirror. Look at the face of that Goddess and tell yourself what you are. Start by saying, "I AM" and follow it with at least five positive words to describe who you are and who you are growing to become.

For example: I AM beautiful, I AM blessed, I AM strong, I AM at peace with myself and the world around me, I AM open-minded, I AM the woman God created me to be.

Now while you are looking yourself in the mirror saying these things, you have to believe them in your heart. These are your words and you have to believe that they are true and they describe everything you are. Your words have power and you have the power to be whatever you want to be. Don't wait on someone to acknowledge you, do it yourself so that when others do it, it will just be confirmation.

It is important to display a positive energy about yourself because people tend to think of you as you think of yourself. Believe that you are. Tell yourself that you are and you will be.

6. PRACTICE POSITIVE THINKING

We need to believe that the Goddess energy within us is real. We have to acknowledge and accept the positive things about ourselves. We have to always acknowledge the positive and appreciate what we have and who we are because we are precious gifts. Once you begin to believe in yourself and your higher power, your abilities are limitless. No matter what happens within your day, always stay positive. Allow the light of love to guide and protect you.

7. CONNECT WITH LIKE- MINDED PEOPLE

It is said that people change every seven or so years, so if that is true our goals, desires and way of thinking all become a little altered, being that we have grown. Every one grows, but we all grow at differently, so it should be clear that sometimes we outgrow some of the people who have been around us for years. It is important to keep moving once you have outgrown someone. Your move is not negative; it is essential as your growth depends on it. We sometimes stay in one area too long because we don't want to let go of someone who is very familiar to us, but are not very beneficial to us. We hold on to boyfriends, girlfriends, best friends and family because we grow accustomed to them, we become comfortable. We also become confused when we start to feel different about being around them because we feel as if they don't understand what we are saying, or doing and the things we once did become redundant. We begin to hunger for more. Change your circle and surround yourself with people who are more like you and what you are growing to become. If you are thinking about being a singer surround yourself with other vocalists, entertainers, musicians. It is not progressive to connect with people who are against your growth, surround yourself with people who are more like you, people who are more positive with an attitude to believe and succeed.

8.MBRACE AND ACKNOWLEDGE YOUR PASSIONS

With the struggles of everyday life and the obstacles that come to deter us, we often get thrown off of course. We sometimes get so caught up in just surviving that we forget to enjoy life. We become overwhelmed with the thoughts of food, clothing, shelter and companionship and we forget to entertain or acknowledge our passions. Our passions, which in many cases, are gifts that come very naturally to us like singing, dancing, writing, reading, architecture, teaching, or whatever, become untapped desires. We end up pursuing other ventures because they pay the bills or they were just easier to obtain, but then we live life with this major void. It is okay to pursue a passion that may take a while before you reap any fruits of your labor. Be true to yourself and go after what you want and do what makes you happy because though that road may be difficult, the journey will be well worth it. Anything worth having is worth working hard for. So, always find a way to entertain and acknowledge your passions, even if you have to do it after you work a job that pays the bills, just find time to free yourself up.

9. SPEND QUALITY TIME WITH YOURSELF

It is very important to take some time for yourself. This time should be spent peacefully so that you can reflect and appreciate all of the things that have taken place in your life. This reflection should happen at least once a day. When you reflect you allow yourself the opportunity to clear the silt. You're life becomes clearer and you become more appreciative. Reflecting creates a space where you can begin to unload some of your baggage and it also allows you time to pat yourself on the back for the things you have accomplished that would otherwise go unnoticed. Reflecting can be done in the park, in the tub, while you take a walk, while you drink a warm cup of tea at your favorite coffee shop or while you rest peacefully in your bed before you go to sleep. It doesn't have to be a long drawn out thing, just give yourself enough time to accomplish what you need to mentally. Being at peace with yourself is a mental thing and reflecting opens the door for peace to enter into your life.

10. SMILE AS OFTEN AS POSSIBLE

I love smiling and I love to see people smiling. It is a certain incredible energy that is released from a person when they smile. It is the most beautiful expression of all. We all notice the effect that a smile has on a person. Have you ever caught yourself walking and it was apparent that you where in a bad mood and someone walked by smiled and asked you how you were doing. You noticed an immediate change in your energy. For that brief moment you felt better. If something that simple could make us feel good just imagine how much good we can do for ourselves and other people, if we just took the time to smile and be polite. It makes us feel good to make others feel good. Smile, it is your shining light, share it with the world and allow people to share theirs with you.

Acknowledging your Goddess power is imperative in this time. Sistars, we must remember, reclaim and reactive our inner Goddesses. The future of Mother Earth depends on it. Light the candle of self love for it will burn bright enough to ignite the love of another.

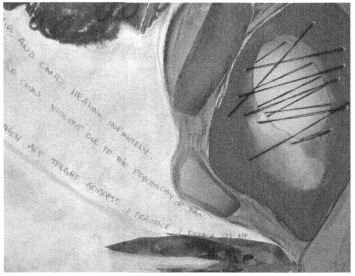

Goddess

By Dail Chambers

7 Healing the Womb

By Rev. Dr. Tonya K. Freeman

Sitting at my computer, deadline quickly approaching, thoughts of my next article begin to flow as I listen to didgeridoo meditation music. The Great Mind of Ma said, "The Spirit of the Womb must be healed." That was my cue as to what my Higher She had to impart.

Many women are in toxic, intimate relationships. These relationships do not allow women to honor themselves, their family, their community or the world at large.

In various Medicine Woman cultures, when a woman has been molested, sexually abused or simply ending an intimate relationship that has run its course, she cleanses herself with a fertile egg,

Saying prayers and affirmations into the egg to release the hurt, the pain, the anguish and to bless the situation, she then passes the egg over the aura of her yoni to absorb the negative energy from her womb,

119

making it an offering to the Great Earth Mother, that She may transform the energy into one of a joyous rebirth.

After cleansing the Spirit of the Womb, one would ask the Mother of the Earth permission to enter into her Sacred Body in order to bury the egg and seal it with salt and ash, as is done amongst the women of the Dagara people in West Africa. This type of ritual cleansing is done four times; four consecutive days, four weeks or four months. Each time another egg is used and the same process of burying the past, is ceremoniously performed.

In other Medicine Woman cultures, they break the egg in running water after such a cleansing.

One can also use crystals instead of eggs. I recommend red, orange or clear quartz crystals for this work. The Earth Mother gives us crystals and gems to work with that we may heal ourselves but She too is in need of a healing and by giving away a crystal to renew and refresh ourselves, we are also helping to renew and refresh Mother Earth.

There are many womb dis-eases that must be healed. It is in this healing that self-love takes place. Women who have experienced womb loss can take that experience and turn it around. When I speak of womb loss, I am talking about any violation that has taken place.

Placing your hands on your belly, spiritually reach inward and become one with your femaleness. Send healing love energy to and acknowledge the vulva. You may very well find yourself becoming poised and powerful. Center yourself by holding your belly, humming your inner song. This simple daily ritual will assist you in your healing process.

All too often we are in a hurry. Running here and there, too busy to slow down. We do not take time to honor our Sacred Womb Space. It is imperative that we make time for a simple ritual that will bring us into a new awareness of ourselves as women. Healing our collective womb, we can begin to journey, exploring the deeper realms of our femaleness. What a joy!

Meditating on the Sacred Vulva while playing a drum to the rhythm of your heart will send rushes of electric impulses to the wounded womb. Beating the drum assists in holding the power of the Spirit of the Womb. The energy from the drum will feel warm like the Sun or cool as river water. Whichever sensation you feel, know that it is doing the work that it was called upon to do. Yin and yang have a complimentary purpose.

Recently, I purchased a small drum and placing it between my legs, I closed my eyes and felt the rhythm of my yoni. I played what I felt and the sound flowed through me taking me into a hypnotic trance. It was good. I've since played many different beats on my drum and each session sends its own healing vibration and rhythm through my body. I enjoy playing my Yoni Healing Drum and recommend it as a practice for those women who have an affinity for the drum. You won't regret it.

The Spirit of the Wounded Womb is yearning for healing love. It has known pain of various degrees. It knows that tender loving care, is a catalyst for being made whole in the Spirit of Love. The Womb Spirit knows and understands the true essence of you and who you are born to be. It wishes for you to remember that as you connect with the Universal Mothers to gain the wisdom so needed in these days.

Become one with your Sacred Gateway. Hold your belly, make a joyous noise and continue the healing process!

8 Divine African Mother Oracle (DAMO)

by Naa Ayele Kumari Maat, PhD, ND, LMT

She is known by 10,000 names... Auset, Isis, Oshun, Yemaya, Mawu, Nut, Black Madonna, Allat, just to name a few. She has been forgotten in history, yet, there she is when we look up into the womb of space. There she is in the depths of the oceans... and yes there she is in the black soil of the earth.... The Divine African Mother. She who has given birth to all that is, has been, or will ever be.

The Great Cosmic Mother begins in this world as the galactic center , from which all life has emerged. This womb, the black hole, has given birth to the Sun, the Moon, all planetary bodies and Stars in our galaxy. In the scriptures, she is referred to "In the beginning" as the darkness, the waters, and the firmament. In the ancient teachings she is the tree of life, the axis mundi, at the center of the universe upon which all heavenly bodies revolve. In Africa, she is the black pot, the cauldron, the calabash, the woven basket, and...the primordial mother of the world.

Manifested in the material realm, she emerges through her human daughters, the African woman who became the progenitor of all human beings on the planet. Everyone can trace their DNA back to her. The oldest bones ever found are those of a woman who lived 4 million years ago in East Africa. Biologically every zygote in the womb is anatomically female first, then mutates to male. This means that biologically, African Females are the most ancient group and gender on the planet. This information is not intended to stir controversy about African women. It is simply   to report the fundamental facts about the African Goddess, and by extension her daughters as mothers to the world.

These facts lead us to realize that the basis of the earliest sciences were those cultivated by African woman. Advances in agriculture and architecture can be traced to the earliest traditions as the first homes via caves, huts and communities were developed from the earlier nomadic lifestyle. Using the movements of objects in the sky to track time and seasons for planting, the science of mathematics emerged along with the first calendars. This led to a greater mapping of the night sky and astronomy was born.

These African women noticed that the moon phases was synchronized to their womb along with the rising tides of the waters. New moons produced a release of blood while children were more likely to be born under full moons. Gynecology and botanical medicine developed out of the relationship with the earth and the natural birthing process. The art of translating science into stories to pass from generation to generation to explain natural phenomenon became the mother of the oral tradition. Eventually, through careful study and observations over thousands of years we came understood the relationship between nature and humanity's experience.

Spiritual practices emerged out of these observations and through intuitive and creative insights, even more realizations came to the foreground. The ancient mothers honored the Goddess as the most ancient artifacts demonstrate thousands of sculptures of ancient goddesses on every continent on the globe the oldest being over 400,000 years old in North Africa. Arts associated with the natural honoring of the Goddess emerged as sculpture, painting, healing, forecasting, and prophesy. African priestesses became revered all over the world as prophetesses, living oracles, and the embodiment of the great mother. Known originally as Kybelles or Cybelles, the Sibylline priestess, along with the Pythias, were consulted by the most prominent world leaders of the time for advice and created a legacy that extends even to this day. Many oracle systems have derived from the science of these prophetesses.

The DAMO (pronounced Dah MO)was inspired by the sciences of the Ancient African mothers and the great Goddesses of Africa who were honored from time immemorial. All oracles were based on a fundamental cosmology or way of viewing the world on a wider scale. It must be understood that the Ancient mothers of Africa accepted both masculine and feminine as complementary opposites in the manifest world. This was reflected more as polarities than just a simplistic view based on gender or judgments of good or bad. Each is interdependent on the other for wholeness. Each is found within the other and both are cosmic twins that were born from the source womb. As in any mother's home, all of her children are loved and accepted just as the all of the sun (stars) and moons all have their home in the womb of space.

The cosmological significance of each one has a role in our ascension process as souls. Essentially, we are moving from the body or solar realm to the lunar realm and back to the stellar realm. Most of our current religions, hierarchies, and traditions are based on the path of the sun. This has manifested as a focus on the outside and external. The Lunar is the path of the heart based on the inner truth. It is self realization and empowerment from within rather than the external manifestation of power. Our path as souls is to move from the outer to the inner and the active to the receptive. From the lunar we will eventually move to the stellar which is based on the essence of who we are.

Ese (Auset/Isis) has this process depicted on her 3 tiered crown. This crown symbolized the throne of the divine and also the path to ascension. The first step was the Earth/ Lunar mysteries, the second step was the celestial world and solar mysteries, and the third and final step to ascension was the stellar mysteries back to the womb. The pope still wears a 3 tiered crown taken from the ancient mothers in Africa.

The DAMO it is based on the lunar mansions which were the earliest calendars. While its use is certainly much older, the earliest was found in Ancient Kemet, and documented to be from 4200 BC. Their oldest calendar consists of 30 days with weeks of 10 producing 360 days. The extra 5 days were considered days outside the normal calendar where the great mother Nut gave birth to 5 new deities.

The lunar mansions are based on the time it takes the moon to complete a full orbit through elliptic. Ancient goddess in Nubia such as Het Hert pronounced (Hether) and Neb-Het reflected these mansions as they names mean mansion of the sun and lady of the mansion respectively. The Skekinah in the Bible is known as she who dwells in the house. It is a mistake to perceive this house as the small dwelling of wood, brick, mud, etc. even though that too was considered a replica of a larger scheme. The mansions, however, is the home of our universe. Each mansion is associated with a particular star and energy vibration.

Every month the moon travels the path through this universe just as the sun does in a year. Women's menstrual cycles are aligned with this very orbit. It is based on 28 to 29.5 days. Our agricultural cycles are also aligned with this cycle. What is visible from the earth is 28 days. What is actual is 29.5. The ancient mothers rounded to 30 not so even days. Each lunar day was a different mansion the moon would travel. At the end, it would have traveled through each forming a circle. Another cycle was notice as well from new moon to new moon

This process is reflective of several concurrent ones within the tradition of the ancient mothers. The first process is the stages of womanhood reflective from new moon to new moon. There is birth, puberty, marriage, motherhood, queenship, sageship or eldership, ancestorhood, then repeating the cycle again through rebirth. This other process is one of spiritual initiation reflective from full moon to full moon. There is a death or descent into emptiness removing all external signs of ego and personality where we face and embrace our shadow at the new moon. Then, our process is a regathering of lost pieces of our divine selves ascending back to wholeness as indicated by the full moon.

The oracle is still in its infancy in terms of development. As it is reflective of active conscious energy in the universe, new information is still being added to understanding it better. As I began the journey of developing it, I found myself experiencing vivid dreams and visions about the stars and lunar mansions upon which it was developed. The ancient mothers fully contributed with vivid messages from the spirit world. Be aware that a more expanded version of the oracle will be explained as the ancient mothers give me the information about them. You will find that as you use it, it will begin to "wake up" and become a conscious tool for your inner and outer life.

One message that was recurrent while I was birthing DAMO was that of logos and the flow of the soul. While this word has floated around in ancient circles for thousands of years, for me it seems to point to process of merging with Spirit into oneness. It is the path of ascension or better described as wholeness. As we journey through each house, we are activating the latent potential of that house's sacred energy within us. There is so much of ourselves that still lay only in its potential form. Wholeness is achieved as we realize that potential and can incorporate it in our being. In other words, we become one with the cosmos, nature and are able to harmonize our lives with it. This is how we birth the inner goddess and become the embodiment of the great mother. We then are able to birth a new earth and higher state of consciousness. It is not the fools journey or the hero's journey. It is the journey of the Mother. It is the journey of a girl to cosmic and goddess consciousness.

For men, the process involves much of the same. It means also to return to the womb of their origin and to finally discover the pot (womb) of gold at the end of the rainbow. So much of the male experience is filled with aggression, and the egoic pursuit of appetites and passions. The need to conquer, rule, and dominate is prevalent. Through the journey to the mother goddess, they find what the hero's journey forgets. That is the power of love and the inner strength of the feminine. It looks like surrender and limitation on the outside. What it is truly is freedom. Every male dominated religion and secret order culminates at the feet of the goddess. Ascension cannot happen without her.

For those that begin to embrace the DAMO, we can begin to use it and allow it to assist us on our souls journey. It is not the only way. It is a way and one that is aligned with the most ancient teachings known to humanity and the African primordial mothers. It does not require initiation or allegiance to foreign deities. You must remember, that those sited in the oracle pages and hetu are inside of you and aspects of the same One. They are parts of your own self whether awakened or not. If you hear them speak or see them in your dream or waking state, know that they are communicating through the oneness of all. We are not separate but expressions of the one source womb... the whole.

How to Make the Oracle

The oracle should be made with as many natural materials as possible. This harmonizes us with nature in its use. It is also best if it is made by the person who will use it so that it is impregnated with their own energy pattern.

Items that can be used to make oracle objects should be no larger than an inch wide and have a flat side so that symbols can be drawn on them Wood chips, round shells, stones or small animal bones are all acceptable. Clay can be formed into objects as well. All are reflections of the earliest African Goddesses. Wood chips reflect her association with the tree of life. Shells reflect the oceans and primal oceans. I made my first set from natural flat round shell 20 mm beads about the size of a penny. Crystals or Stones especially black ones or lapis, reflect the earliest seats or thrones of power. The canvas of the most ancient writings are found on caves and stones over 30,000 years ago. The clay is reflective of the mother earth.

In any case, you should have 30 of them. Later editions of this oracle may contain more but for beginners, 30 is what we will use. 30 is for each lunar day. They are referred to as Het (pronounced Hey) hetu (plural) , huts, houses, or mansions. Each will symbolize a different mansion of the sky.

A paint marker or fine tip permanent marker may be used to draw the symbols. For those that are savvy with a knife or paint brush, they may be chiseled on or painted on. I am not that savvy so I used marker. One symbol should be painted on each item. Feel free to modify or change the symbol if you feel inclined or you connect with another symbol to represent the energy. Adinkra symbols or symbols from an African syllabary may work better for you. There are no hard and fast rules here. If there is something that resonates more with your spirit, go with it. This oracle is for you and must speak to you on an inner level.

Allow the items that have been painted on to dry and use clear acrylic spray to seal it. This way they symbols wont rub off with continued use. Once they are complete, they are ready for use but it is best if you can consecrate under the full moon. Other ways to consecrate them is to wash them in river, lake, or sea water with a drop of your blood. Or, a simple prayer or libation may do to consecrate your oracle.

The hetu may kept in a black pouch, a navy pouch with stars, a calabash or gourd, a bowl, basket, or pot with a lid. These containers symbolize the great womb from which all things and wisdom comes. As we pull one out, the womb is giving birth to the symbols and signs of that house. Sometimes herbs and other sacred items are added to the womb such as a lock of hair, crystals, herbs or roots, etc. It really is up to you. Keep the oracle in a sacred and clear space so as not to contaminate the energy. It can be portable and go with you, or it can be in a stationary place.

DAMO oracle on flat 20mm shell

How to use the DAMO

While there are several ways to use this oracle, only one will be covered within the context of this writing. Before anything, establish a connection with the source. A prayer of libation with fresh water, wine, or gin is helpful. Singing can also be done as well as ringing a bell. This helps to call the Mother's attention. If you are on the go, just make a connection in your heart by being still for a moment. When satisfied, simply ask a question and draw out a house. Draw 2 if you need clarity. The two will complement one another. It is best to avoid yes or no questions and ask more open ended questions. It is also important to remember that while this oracle may answer mundane questions, it is designed to respond to your soul's calling, not your ego. The answers are varied and you may need to sit and meditate on them as you receive them. You can use the symbol and the name of it as a visualization tool and mantra to focus the energy in your meditation. After a while, using and understanding them will become second nature and you won't need to refer to the book. For now, get to know the ancient mother's presented and how they show up in your world. Expect to be surprised! For those that are interested, the first question I asked this oracle was what energy was governing it. I received Sati, Sothis, Sophia which speaks of divine guidance from your higher self and other worlds!

Open ended questions to ask: Fill in the ...
What is the energy for the day? Week? Month? Year?
How do I approach...?
What is my soul lesson/ purpose in ...?
Advise on ...

Example Opening Prayer

Divine African Mother
Sacred Source of all things seen and unseen and all things to all people.
From the cosmic womb of the Black hole to the Mother Earth and into my own Sacred Womb,
 I invoke your name of many names...
The music of the spheres and the song of stars...
I open my heart to receive your wisdom.
I open my eyes that I may see clearly
I open my womb that I birth truth in your oracle.
With gratitude and reverence,

I seek guidance in the matter of.......

Ask your question....

References

4 million old woman
> http://news.nationalgeographic.com/news/2009/10/091001-
> oldest-human-skeleton-ardi-missing-link-chimps-ardipithecus-
> ramidus.html

400,000 year Goddess Sculpture in North Africa
> http://news.bbc.co.uk/2/hi/science/nature/3047383.stm

Mami Wata: Africa's Ancient God/dess Unveiled by Mama Zogbe

DAMO

(Divine African Mother Oracle) Interpretations

By Ayele Kumari Maat

Uche / Aje (Igbo/ Yoruba)

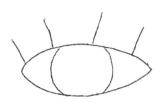

Key Concepts: **Conception, Potential Energy, New Idea Appropriate Use of Will**
Zodiac: Aries
Part of Body: Head, Forehead, Eye

This is conception and awakening. = This is where everything comes from the spiritual world into the material world. It is a new idea, initiation or a rebirth of something that went away. Calls for meditation on source and establishing intention for what you want to manifest into the world. New Moon ---great creative power in which good planning is necessary. A time to easily manifest what you want so be careful of thoughts and only focus on what you want. Iyami Aje were the wise women of the forest where women sought healing, herbs, etc. This energy of Aje is natural to every woman. it indicates spiritual power from your mother's

137

line. Men became afraid of this power because they couldn't control. Yet they had to respect it. Throughout Africa, the mother has the power to curse or bless. To this end, since this power is so strong, focus only on loving happy thoughts and bless others with your Aje. Ancestors and Spiritual guides can support this situation. A good time for spiritual cleansing and forgiving of past.

Nne Ala/ Ani (Igbo)

Key Concepts: **Creation, Pregnancy, Patience, Planning, Trust**
Zodiac:Taurus
Part of Body: Yoni, neck

Nne Ala is the Ibo Mother goddess who governs fertility of land and laying down the laws of life. This is creative energy. It is the gestation of things developing but not yet ripe. Requires patience and the need to support and nurture as in a pregnancy. Things require a gradual development and step by step process and is a time for planning and preparation -- Moon rising above the horizon after New Moon. One of the sign is a horn of plenty indicating a prosperous time with an abundance of choice and all needs being met. A time to improve diet and build body. Just after completing this Oracle, Nne Ani appeared to me to help me with a healing tool for a friend. It was intended to

138

create a new heart by making a doll and placing a heart inside. Just after, this friend got a message that her heart was spontaneously healing and her heart was creating new arteries…a process called arteriogenesis. So Nne Ala can be called upon for healing and renewal. She told me she could be called Ala or Ani.

Tanit (Libya)

Key Concepts: **Birth, Emergence, Manifestation, Take Action**

Zodiac: Taurus

Part of Body: Integumentary System (skin)

Tanit (Libya) was known as the weaver of life and This is birth and the emergence of things that become visible and manifested. It says take action. This is a sign that is leaping into action and going for it! Here we have the birth and that which you want has arrived. Now we are beyond guessing and wondering and we know. Tanit says things are cooking up and its smelling good. We have been born and freed from the womb. New experiences are pouring forth.

Hethert (Nubia)

Key Concepts: **Growth, Chariot or Vehicle for Ascension, Values,**

139

Zodiac: Taurus

Part of Body: Breast

Het Hert (Egypt) Tree of life. This is a place of major growth and evolution. It says look at your foundation, values. Discard that which is unworthy and step onto higher ground. Your life will reflect your values. Can also reflect your body as your temple. Examine the foundation of your life. -- Help from your Ancestors and Guides are indicated. The chariot is also a sign and reflective of a vehicle. This vehicle can indicate your body, your car, or a tool for spiritual growth. We have learned how to use our body vehicle and are starting to walk and learn. This sign also speaks to our senses and things that affect our senses. We must be sure to use them but not to be a slave to them as we are more than just a body.. We are immortal souls.

Athene

Key Concepts: **Truth, Innocence, Communication and Learning**

Zodiac: Taurus/ Gemini

Part of the Body: Throat

Athene (Libya) carried a blade of justice indicating coming to a truth or learning something new. It speaks to the need for strategy, study, and creatively solving problems. She speaks of innocence and keeping an open mind to new possibilities. There is a new learning phase and respect for the teachers are important. Creativity is strong here and great skill and ability in the arts are noted. Speaking your truth also comes up for this sign.

Seshet

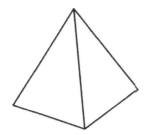

Key Concepts: **Mind, Awareness, Higher Reasoning**
Zodiac: Gemini
Part of the Body: Brain/ Nervous system Psyche
Seshet(Egypt) was known as the first architect and mathematician as she is attributed with establishing the plans for pyramids to be built. By extension, she laid the plans for the universe and our life's journey. This symbol speaks to being clear, using high reasoning and the higher mind. Focus on positive thoughts and the need for clear thinking. Media and communication avenues can be influences here. Because the focus is on buildings the environment may need to be addressed as well as a need to harmonize the environment. This may be the environment in your home or the outer environment. Education is important during this time. Learn as much as you can for Information is power...and money!

Anuket Eshu

Key concepts: **Crossroads, Opportunity, Duality, Trustworthiness, Laughter, the arts**

Zodiac: Gemini

Part of the Body: Respiratory System

Anuka Eshu (Derived from Egypt to W. Africa) is the mother of the crossroads and all other crossroad deities. Crossroads are places in life where choices are made. May represents doorway and pathways. Here, the symbol is of the river crossroads and Anuke from Ancient Kemet. Anuke became Anuka Esue in the West. There is a choice to be made and growth comes through challenges. You are encountering soul lessons that are designed for you to grow. Evaluate perceptions, review, and renew your views. Creative abundance can be found by taking new paths in life. Can also speak to the ability to create wealth and abundance. Watch for nervous energy and anxiety. Journaling may help you. It also says be trustworthy in all of your dealing and watch for trustworthiness in others. In another vain, the arts and creativity is emphasized. Laughter, children, and open doors are all signs. Let your words express your greatest intent and pay attention to details.

Yemaya/ Emme Ya

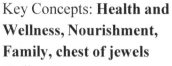

Key Concepts: **Health and Wellness, Nourishment, Family, chest of jewels**
Zodiac: Cancer
Part of Body: Stomach, Digestive

Nourishment is important with this symbol. The food that is eaten, medicine, and what we nourish ourselves with. It says to be sure you are nourishing your mind, body, and spirit with things that will keep you well and offer longevity. Indicates a strong harmonious support. This speaks to realizing the source of your support and needs is the universe. Your family, relationships, and close community bonds offer a wealth of resources and prosper. This also speaks to drawing energy from your spiritual well and returning to the essentials. We are learning to cook and care for ourselves properly during this stage of development. Listen to your dreams and get plenty of sleep.

Watchet

Key Concepts: **Kundalini, Emotions, Feelings, Sexual Potency**
Zodiac: Cancer
Part of the Body: Endocrine System/ Spinal column
Wadjet (Egypt) This is the

143

origin of the word witch. It is spiritual power and the kundalini. This symbol is an ancient version of the caduceus used as a symbol for healing. Through merging opposites, a synchronistic whole can occur. This is strong emotional energy that must be channeled properly. Doing so can lead to healing addictions, illusions, unhealthy attachments. It speaks to a breakthrough and ability to transmute stagnate or difficult situations to make major progress. There is no going back...only forward! This is powerful emotional energy and high sensitivity. Watchet warns to not use this energy recklessly and to not revert back to old patterns that can undermine your progress. This energy contains feelings and emotions. This energy can also involve the merging of opposites and sexual potency.

Nekebet/Mut
Key Concepts:
**Leadership,
Dominion, Crown,
Maturity**

Zodiac: Between Cancer and Leo , Star Sirus
Part of Body: Blood

Mut/Nekebet is here. She is the vulture that every queen is crowned with in ancient Kemet. All great mothers and queens are crowned with a bird or known by one. This is Nekebet's legacy. Mut is the Grandmother and matriarch. She is the Goddess of Queens. Every goddess has a bird associated with her and this dates back to Mut. The ancient crowns were associated with birds and feathers. This speaks to leadership and taking charge. This also speaks to the courage to stand for what is right and to lead is to serve. Here we take dominion over our lives. We also take responsibility for our actions and mature. This sign can teach you how to be comfortable with yourself.

Auset, Eset, Isis, Nana Esi, Asase Ya

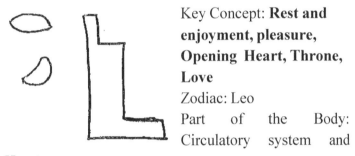

Key Concept: **Rest and enjoyment, pleasure, Opening Heart, Throne, Love**
Zodiac: Leo
Part of the Body: Circulatory system and Heart

Here is Esi as she is called throughout the continent. Here stands the path of the heart. There are those who follow the path of the head with its analytical reasoning and left and right paths. Here it is the middle path of the heart. She tells us to listen to the heart which is the seat of the soul. Here is where the hidden sun lies. It is the throne of the goddess and it is made of love. At this left breast, this sun is fed the power of love and is nurtured with life giving energy. She is listening to the mothers intuition in her heart.

145

Because this energy reminds us to open our hearts, it also promotes the energy of relationship, union as you seek to connect lovingly with others. To that end, marriage, wives, and mothers. are supported.

Shekmet/ Shekinah

Key Concepts: **Divine Revelation, Personal Empowerment, Strength**

Zodiac: Leo

Part of Body: Immune System / Breath

Shekmet (pronounced Shekma and also spelled Sekhmet) means powerful mother in Egypt and Nubia and she teaches feminine power. She is a mother lion who brings a purifying fire burning away all that ails you. She is divine breath and the master healer as she triggers the electromagnetic energy to flow through the body. This sign is illuminating like a lightning bolt. It brings the purification of thoughts and answered prayers but calls for balancing this power with mercy and love. This is the big mama that don't play but loves strong. She can also bring healing through energy methods and powerful medicine. As a mother lioness, she brings the protection strength to the weak and karmic correction to those who have strayed from the path.

146

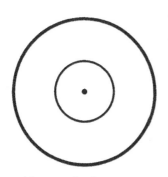

Abrewa   primordial   mother Akan

Key Concepts: **Full Moon or Full Sun, Fullness, Abundance**
Zodiac: Virgo
Part of the Body: Full Breasts

Abrewa is the power to manifest what one. This carries the full moon energy and with it the ability to manifest what you seek. Everything is accentuated here and an enormous amount of energy and resources are present. We are fully realizing our power now. This speaks of abundance. It could be an abundance of spiritual power, money, wealth, etc. When you get this sign, you will be provided for and what you wish to do will be successful.

Sati, Sothis, Soptet, Sophia

Key concepts: **High Priestess, Mysteries, Purity, Wisdom**
Zodiac: Virgo
Part of Body: Pituitary

This is the High Priestess the diamond, black dove, and the holy spirit. Also known as Sophia, Sothis and Sati in Nubia. This sign speaks to great gifts and resources available. It suggests the need to also have enough to share with others. The high priestess guides others and has attained mastery in something. It speaks to channeling divine guidance from the higher self and other worlds. Oracles, sacred texts , or someone who is an expert in their field may offer assistance. This speaks to relying entirely on the source and holding on to your light. You may have forgotten your true power and who you truly are. This sign reminds you of the divine immortal being you are and to sing your song proudly and with confidence as this sign affirms the use of words of power to create magic. You are ordained from on high. This sign brings great wisdom.

Mami Wata, Nne Ani, Ogbuide, Olokun

Key Words: **positive change, renewal, resurrection, discernment**
Zodiac: Virgo / Libra
Part of the Body: Intestines

The water goddesses of ancient Africa hold the python as sacred along with the power of the ocean. Mermaids are prominent as well and can symbolize the balancing of our watery emotions with the stability of the earth. Renewal is major theme along with immortality. The snake renews through the shedding of old skin. When it bites its own tail, it symbolizes no beginning or ending and a perfect circle. The coils that spiral reflect the spiral of live from the milky way to our finger tips. The snake coils and speaks to the cosmology of the universe and the ancient women's wisdom. African women would make baskets that coiled or spiraled. In fact this oracle is based on Mehen, an oracle that is at least 7000 years old in East Africa. It is a coiled snake with 28-36 sections depending on who and when it was created. The snake was not always seen as evil as in the Judeo Christian interpretation. In fact, the snake is considered wise as it is the oldest part of our anatomy and is linked to our spine and nervous system. It speaks to the power of renewal through shedding old skin. It can also speak to spiritual mastery through the "serpent" in our spine.

Maat

Key concept: **soul purpose, Balance, moderation, order, truth**
Zodiac: Libra
Part of the Body: Kidneys
Maat (Egypt) is the mother of truth, balance, order. This sign is aligned is aligned with living truth. This truth is more about

universal truth and your souls purpose. Maat asks you to manifest your authentic self. This means living your truth without the need for approval. TRUTH is The Real Understanding That Heals. Often we see truth as either this or that, black or white, male or female. Truth is neither and all, and relative to situation. It requires a balancing of all opposites and moderation in all things. Here is the dance of the balancing of the poles. As you seek to manifest your souls destiny, it is important that you look at the work beyond just personal gratification and more to personally evolve you and or your community. Maat also speaks of listening to your conscience. Make sure that you use integrity and honor in your interactions.

Oshun/ Osun
Key Concept: **Harmony, Attraction, Sensuality, Beauty and Joy, Music, Fellowship**
Zodiac: Libra/ Scorpio
Part of the Body- Pancreas/ Vaginal canal
Oshun is the social butterfly of West Africa and the Diaspora. Powerful mother of the rivers, she teaches us how to go with the flow of life with joy, the arts, inner beauty and love. This ability usually attracts others to us through our willingness to relate. To that end, love, union, relationships, sexuality, and new opportunities.

This sign crowns us with success in these areas. It also speaks to what we deserve based on what we have done. This sign acts as a mirror to reflect what we are putting out to others. This is the more you give, the more you receive.

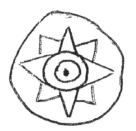

Inanna

Key Concepts: **Decrease, Release, limitation, Conflict, Contraction**
Zodiac: Scorpio
Part of the Body: Muscular System
This sign is one of contraction as the contractions that may happen while giving birth. There may be a decrease, feeling restricted, or feeling limited in ability. It could also speak to a need to release people or perceptions that no longer serve your growth. It is important to watch for jealousy or betrayal or some other sting that may unsettle you . It can be the medicine in an illness. Homeopathy may help. Homeopathy brings healing by the law of what can kill can heal. There may be a pending battle. It could be inner or outer. It is likely to impact some area you are most vulnerable. This sign brings protection and assurance that you will be fine. You are assured that any perceived loss at this time is designed to move you more toward a greater possibility. It is best not to resist and to just let go.

This sign may also bring muscle tension and the need for massage to release contracted muscles and relieve stress.

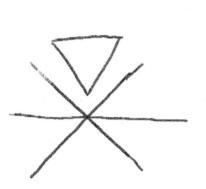

Kali

Key Concepts:
Dissolution Magic mystery, Descent, Surrender, Tower, Letting Go
Zodiac: Scorpio
Part of Body: Colon/ Liver

Here we plunge into our shadow selves where any illusions we may have had are cast away forever. Here we get to the root of the situation. This requires dealing with core issues. This is deep subconscious and core healing. Sometimes things have to be broken down in order for us to see the pieces clearly. This speaks to all of the pieces we may have left behind because of trauma and the need to retrieve them and embrace them again. Release old fears, insecurities, and false fronts. There is nothing to fear but fear itself. Put your faith now in the transforming power of Spirit. It is the final elimination of our fears for good. The illusions and trap set forth by the ego can finally be dissolved and our goddess selves can emerge and take flight. Here you will choose between the lower and higher.

Ngame

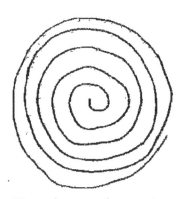

Key Concepts: **Regeneration, Turning Point, Wheel of fortune, Cosmic law transformation, wounded healers**

Zodiac: Ophiuchus

Part of the Body: Hormones

There is a need to understand spiritual laws and cycles of life. With this house, extraordinary energy and success is indicated. There may have been a down turn that had happen and now things are on the upswing again. This house is also concerned with global and community wide situation. Here catering to humanity and the big picture is emphasized. There is also a need to transform something from one thing to another. Like corn or wheat to bread or gin. This is a process of refinement and alchemical transformation.

Oya

Key Concept: **Bravery, Courage, Winds of change, Positive Revolution, rainbow after the storm**

Zodiac: Sagittarius

Part of the Body: Legs

Oya brings transformative change and victory in this situation. This change may act within our being as a great illumination that changes our experience forever or it may bring the courage to forge forth in your truth with the assurance of being supported by divine guidance. This energy is like a lightning bolt and power line. Be sure to use great wisdom in this situation and defer to wise counselors, and guidance as this house bring assured success blessed by the ancients. This can also speak to warrior energy, Amazons, and suggest that you stay the course. Masculine energy may also be indicated.

Mawu/ Nana Buruku (Bouclou-Buluku)

Key Concepts: **glory wisdom and honor and Recognition, achievement**

Zodiac: Sagittarius /Capricorn

Part of Body: Bones

High value and worth. Great Power is in this house as well as elders with great wisdom. Here things are presented on a platform. There is something or someone on display. It is time to accept recognition for your achievement and recognize others. Honor and accolades come with this sign Bright light and being exalted in

154

some way. Here we raise the great mother in the form of Nana and Mawu. These are some of the most ancient mothers and the great grandmothers of the spirit. The sounds Ma and Na and slight variations of the vowels are the prelude to the majority of references to mother. They are wise beyond comprehension and established the laws by which all of existence came to be. When she speaks.....you better listen and pay attention. It is also a message that to lead is to serve.

Egun/ Aakhu

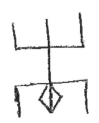

Key Concepts: **Connection, Family line, Humanity, Ancestors**
Zodiac: Capricorn
Part of the Body: DNA, genetic makeup
Protection, libations wealth hearing. There are ancestors and guides present in this situation. We are the sum total of those who came before. This is our greater family and genetic history. Blood and DNA play a role. The ancestors offer guidance in our dreams and waking state. This is a day of the great ancestral mothers and it calls for honoring them. These are the great ancestors who changed our world and have transcended. The ancient priestess of 10000 years ago. The ancient living oracles. We are one and not separated Pouring libations and making food offerings is a way to offer them substance in the

etheric realm so that they can impact our world of matter more effectively. In this way they can help you and offer you assistance. By offering prayers and libations to them, you assist them with their journey on the other side. You offer life energy to them as support. Stage of development: Community Elder or Sage

Allat

Key Concepts:
abundance and reputation, Increase, Resources
Zodiac: Capricorn
Part of Body: Cellular

Wealth or increase may accompany this sign. An attitude of gratitude help you to share the wealth with others. The reputation tends to play a role here and how things appear. Be sure not to get to attached or distracted by superficiality. Hard work produces permanent wealth. Be sure to be fiscally responsible with funds This house brings strength and concrete achievements. Real Estate and solid investments are favored. Business Partnerships, unions and things having to do with children are highly supported here. Blessings abound.

Nut

Key Concepts: **Glowing Healing Power , tortoise shell, Bowls, Primal Waters**

Zodiac: Aquarius

Part of the Body: Lymph

Nut Pronounced Nu is the heavens and noted by her body of stars. Here is the source of all and all blessings stream forth from Nu. When a soul has completed their journey on earth, it is to this Mother of Heaven you return. Therefore Nut is the source of all wealth, blessings, and peace. It calls for a time of inner peace, calm, and contemplation to receive the greatest source of life. It calls for faith and prayer as it is often a time of struggling through or overcoming challenges. Realize that any perceived mistakes now can be understood as lessons and calls for us to return to our great mother for support. This is a time of massive healing.

Hekat / Hekate

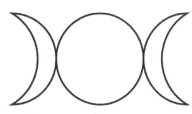

Key Concepts: **Detachment, Profound Understanding, Death and Rebirth**

Zodiac: Aquarius

157

Part of the Body: Lower Legs/ Feet

Hekat are very primordial mothers who governs the swampy areas of our lives. She is the tadpole that transforms into a frog. Frogs also a symbol in this house due to its ability to change from tadpole to frog and navigate both worlds. This is speaking to the ability to navigate the spiritual world with the material. It means an initiation and evolution is taking place. Here we also find Hekat who is also known as Hekate in European circles though she is not at all considered heinous as described in European literature. Hekat is the old mother and midwife for babies and the soul. She is responsible for birthing you into a new state of consciousness as indicated by the frog. She eventually became Hekate a crossroad goddess because she stands at the crossroads of life and death. Within the name Hekat is Heka which speaks to the magical power of sound and its ability to magically transform anything. In this house, we are cutting through and shifting consciousness where we can navigate greater terrain. We are cleaning up our act and getting it together.

Black Madonna / Fatima

Key Concepts: **Hidden, Stillness, Meditation, Overcoming fears**
Zodiac: Pisces
Part of the Body: Labia and Pubis

158

The Black Madonna is often veiled. This veil is not to a symbol of subservience but one of hidden mystery and knowledge. There is a need to peel back the layers to receive the keys to the mystery. Here, we delve into the deep waters of the unknowable. A woman's vagina has 7 natural veils. Pubic hair, outer labia, inner labia, clitoral hood, pubic bone, Hyman, and vaginal opening.

Fatima showed up to me while developing this oracle She showed me who she truly is...the eye of the sun that is veiled from common eyes. While prominent in Islam, she goes back to pre Islamic Sudan as the heroine Goddess, Fatna or Fatma. Fatna veiled herself to prevent unworthy men from seeing her superficially. The Islamic hijab, burkha and the Habit worn by nuns are a remnant of this ancient form of the dark mother. It was not seen as a form of subservience in its original form. It represented a hidden treasure. The temples of Nut and Isis all said that " I am that which was, which is, and which ever will be. No mortal man has ever lifted my veil and survived. These statues are always veiled. This is the blackness that you see when you close your eyes. Also it is the Sun at midnight. There in the darkness and stillness, might you find visions and dreams that reveal to you the mystery of what is hidden. This sign ask you to still your unruly emotions and thoughts and find what lies beneath the surface of your experience. It speaks of removing veils to know the truth. There is hidden treasure there, not in what you believe you see. It also speaks to unveiling your authentic self...that which is beyond illusions.

Gbadu/ Oduduwa/ Iya Agbe

Key Concepts: **Depth and Spiritual discipline, inner voice, Dreams, Higher Consciousness, Wisdom, Big Picture**

Zodiac: Pisces

Part of the Body: Eyes/ Pineal Gland

Holy Daughter and the Sage within. She is our inner oracle and voice of the Divine. There is a need for higher truth, spiritual consciousness, and detached wisdom. The ancients saw this as Maati the 3 truths. It is something like your side, my side and then the truth. Gbadu is the goddess that represents the Afa oracle and sits at the top of the tree of life. Having 16 eyes, she could see everything. She is known as Egbe or Oduduwa in Ifa, the supreme mother of the calabash or womb. This is a good time to talk to a life coach ,priestess, or spiritual master. Or, you can work on spiritual development and seeking wisdom.

Neb-Het/ Ninhavanhu-Ma

Key Concepts:
Transcendence, Law of love, Acceptance,
Zodiac: Pisces
Part of the Body: Chakras
This is a sign of the sacred heart and transcending the entire experience. Surrender comes with this sign and resolution. Cleanse and purge. It brings deliverance. It calls for you to be joyous and to not be sad... you are divinely guided. This is the place of where you are evaluating yourself for purity of intent and action. You are no longer dependent on outer sources but that which is within as the entire source of your every want need or desire. This is the greatest of wisdom and becoming the embodiment of wisdom. This asks, what is your greatest truth that you know for sure with no one ever needing to tell you. It also speaks to tolerance, compassion, and understanding of others who may not be where you are or may perceive something different than you. Judgment is discarded here as we realize that we all struggle with something and have had challenges. We are not better or worse than anyone else and in fact there is no need to compete as one better than the other. Within, there is a need to release harsh self-judgment of ourselves. In the larger picture, we have chosen certain experiences to help us

161

grow and learn... and we did. We now transcend the mystery of a world of duality. Stage of development: Re balancing of alter egos and more soul driven than body.

World Womb/ Cosmic Calabash/ Sacred Egg

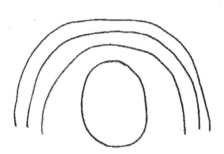

Key Concepts:
Goddess /
Cosmic
Consciousness,
Law of One
Zodiac: Space/
Stellar/   Supernal
Light

Part of the Body: Womb and Fallopian tubes, Ovaries
The womb is where we experience our first love. This sign reminds to love, forgive, offer penance, and a spiritual initiation to transition into the next phase of life. It is a time of clearing any remnants of karmic debt and to ask and give forgiveness. Give joy and surrender the ego completely as you return to the womb of conscious and are made whole. Here, the journey of the soul comes full circle and wholeness of the mind body and soul are united into one. We have transcended our human limitations and achieved wholeness. We are of one consciousness and illuminated. This calls for the greatest of character. Stage of development: Returning to source.

Dancing Lady
By Alisa Kuumba Zuwena

9 Honoring Our Ancestors

by Alisa Kuumba Zuwena

Inuit Tradition

In 1998, I was introduced to a simple ancestral ceremony by an Inuit Shaman by the name of Grey Wolf at a spiritual retreat in North Georgia. It was a remote area on land owned by a lovely couple. This enabled us to be totally free in performing ceremony. There was no interference of hearing the hustle and bustle of city life, just the sounds of nature. The ceremony was simple, yet very powerful. In this tradition, the ancestors are fed items of food into a burning fire. It is said, that if the fire cracks and pops, it's your ancestors speaking to you.

In our ceremony, there were some people who needed to connect with their ancestors as there were no sounds at all. With some of us, the fire crackled and popped to the point of bringing laughter in their conversation with us.

Before honoring the ancestors, we began by smudging with sage and sweet grass. There are many ways of doing this. Some people choose to smudge the face only, while others choose to smudge the whole body. We then quieted centered ourselves. There was very little conversation. We decided on the foods we would like to offer to the ancestors. Being of African-American descent, I chose foods that I knew my ancestors enjoyed.

We had the pleasure of having a huge stone fireplace in the lodge where we were staying. We circled around the hearth and began ceremony. We began with a traditional song by Grey Wolf. One by one we offered food to our ancestors. Suddenly, the room felt as if there were 100's of people in the room. In other words the room felt full, yet there were probably less than 20 of us doing ceremony. There were many dreams that night. That is a good sign as that is the way the ancestors can communicate well with us on this plane. So that was an indication of a successful ceremony and a confirmation of their accepting the offerings. That night we learned a new chant/song, which is sung when a community gathering has taken place. It is a call and response chant. It doesn't mean goodbye. It means until we meet again.

I have written it phonetically below: Ee-Ay-

Ehhhhhhh
Ee-Ay-Ehhhhhhh

Ah-Ahhhhhhh Ah-
Ahhhhhhh

He haw, he haw, Hy ahhway
He haw, he haw, Hy ahhway

Akan Tradition

Preparing the Ancestral Altar:

Set aside space (may be mantel piece, shelf, table, etc;)
Place photos, mementos, treasures, favored items, etc; of your Ancestors. Use a white candle and light when making offerings, prayer or meditation. Offer meals, snacks, hard candy, fruit, flowers or any things that were favored by your Ancestors.
DO NOT LEAVE CANDLE LIT WHEN NOT AT HOME

Purchase a new setting of dishes (white or clear) for serving the Ancestors. (Plate, saucer, cup, bowl and glass)

On Thursdays (day set aside for the Ancestors) prepare the following and offer alone or with the meal of the day:

Light the candle and give thanks.

Ingredients
(Combine the following)

Fine White Corn Meal
Chopped Onions
Cayenne Pepper
(If desired, canned or fresh fish may also be added)
Add boiling water and mix together well.
Form patties and fry in Vegetable or Corn Oil.
Every 40 days Kweisidah is observed in honor of the Ancestors.

Prepare the following:

White Yams
Boiled Eggs
Palm Oil
Peel and cut into cubes, boil and mash Yams.
Leave 1/2 of the yams plain. Shape into balls.
The other 1/2 of the yams, mix with the palm oil.
To prepare the palm oil, slice medium onion and fry in palm oil. Strain the oil (discard the onions, or add to a stew if you happen to be cooking) and add to the other

1/2 of the boiled yams. Mix thoroughly and shape into balls. Serve the boiled eggs and yams together.

Light the candle. Pour libation and give thanks and honor your Ancestors.
NOTE: DO NOT USE SALT WHEN PREPARING FOOD FOR THE ANCESTORS

African-American Ancestral Ceremony

I have discovered as many spirit children in the Americas, ways of honoring our ancestors. I embrace the ancestors born in this land, and the other blood lines of my people. I also embrace the ancestors that travel with me, that are not linked in my bloodline.

My great-grandmother on my father's side of the family was Cherokee. Her name was Rozena Brown. She married a Black man at the turn of the 20th century. They moved to the pan-handle of Florida in a horse driven wagon. They were blessed with many children. My Grandmother, Mariah Foster and my great aunts are really a reflection of the Native American blood. They are very red and have the texture of hair indicative of the Native American peoples.

I am also aware of the Caucasian bloodline. I believe my mother's side of the family is connected to the Scottish people. Her maiden name was Donaldson.

Ancestral Altar/Shrine Set-up

There is a lot of ways to set up your ancestor shrine. I embrace many traditions and my ancestor shrine reflects that. It is a personal decision, although there are common factors in all ancestral shrines that holds and builds the power.

Items Needed:

White Candle
White Cloth or White Lace Cloth
Photos of Ancestors
List of Ancestors who you do not have photographs
Favorite items of the Ancestor(s)
White or Clear Bowl of Water
Favorite food(s) (Leave on Shrine for 24 hours, then dispose)
Flowers
Sage and or Frankincense & Myrrh
Bell

Directions:

Ring a bell 7 times before praying or continuously during your prayers as pouring libation. Directions on how to pour libation is in the next paragraph.

Pouring Libation
Sprinkle or pour water on a living plant or the ground and say: "I'd like to honor the Ancestors of the Land, of the Blood and of the Spirit". You may continue honoring your Ancestors by calling or thinking their names, while pouring water after each name on the plant or ground.

Honoring the Ancestors with Song

Sing songs from your Ancestors time on earth. For instance, for African-Americans, sing old time Spirituals or songs that you know your Ancestor loved.

Below are suggestions for our African-American Ancestors.

Ancestor's Breath
by Sweet Honey and the Rock Original

Listen more often to things than to beings
Listen more often to things than to beings

Tis the ancestor's breath
When the fire's voice is heard

Tis the ancestor's breath
In the voice of the waters

Ahhhh…whish….ahhh…whish….ahhh…whish

Those who have died have never ever left
The dead have a pact with the living…..

They are in the mother's breast
They are in the wailing child
They are with us in our homes
They are with us in a crowd
The dead have a pact with the living

Listen more often to things than to beings
Listen more often to things than to beings

Tis the ancestor's breath
When the fire's voice is heard
Tis the ancestor's breath
In the voice of the waters

Chant from Ghana (Multi Praise Chant for Honoring
the Living and the Dead, and Accomplishments)
Heni wani wani
Heni wani wani Oooohhhhhh

Heni wani wani
(Say person's name you are honoring)
OOOOHHHHHHH

For those who have recently passed on
Wole' Wa Egungun
Wole' Wa

Oshun- I work a lot with Osun as a artist. Osun is
the Mother of the Rivers, Women, and Prosperity. She
is a Goddess that known throughout West Africa and
the Diaspora. She is called to attract Love, Harmony,
and Prosperity

Mama Oshun Recipe for Attracting Love and Prosperity

Five Oranges/Tangerines or Five slices of
Oranges/Tangerines
Cinnamon, Cloves, Cardamom, Honey
Five Tuberose or Honeysuckle Votive Candles
White or Clear Plate
Vase of Yellow Roses or Yellow Daffodils

Attract Love and Harmony
Osun Chant - Iya Mi Ile' Odo (Mother of the Rivers)

Ide' were' were'
Ide' were' were'

Nita Osun

Ide' were' were'
Ide' were' were'
Nita Osun

Cheke' cheke'
Nita ya

Ide' were' were'
Ide' were' were'
Nita Osun

Alisa Kuumba's Floral Cleansing Waters for cleaning your Aura

1 Gallon of Distilled Water
Dried or fresh rose petals
Dried of fresh lavender flowers
3 drops of lavender essential oil
5 drops of honeysuckle essential oil
7 drops of jasmine essential oil
6 drops of frankincense essential oil
Few drops of Rum and Gin or Anisette (spirit of this water)

Place the cleansing waters in a large calabash, wooden bowl or white/clear bowl.

Place your hands in the water and lightly sprinkle these waters on your head and mimic washing your whole body including your feet.

Invocation before use

Healing waters, cleansing waters, ancient waters........Heal us, bless us with your loving, nurturing and compassionate element of life!

Items needed for Ritual
Tree branches with leaves tied with purple and red string
Efun or Benzoin clay powder
Floral Waters (See in recipe section)
Rum or Gin
Cigars
3 Coconuts
Fresh Fruit for the Shrine
Sage
Frankincense and Myrrh
Lavender, Jasmine and Gardenia incense

Preparation:
3 women must create sacred space in ritual/ceremony area.

These three women are to cleanse the women with floral waters, and smudge them with sage before they can enter the sacred space of Ritual/Ceremony.

Note: These women will cleanse each other after cleansing all the women.

10 Initiation: A Journey

By Tonya K. Freeman

Many years ago there was an awakening of the Divine Femi9 Energy within a young girl. She felt a need to connect with a deeper, more profound part of herself as she journeyed along the path to her Soul Essence. She was only seven years old at the time, which is considered to be the age of reason in American society. A voice whispered, "You are here on Earth to attain your highest spiritual good." She looked into the mirror and saw her Soul. The beauty of it brought a smile to her lips that she felt in her heart.

As Daughter of the Rainbow grew up within the society in which she lived, she had drifted along various paths in life that were a series of initiations unbeknownst to her. All the while she was being prepared for a great work. Having been brought up a Catholic, she was exposed to the Goddess in the person of the Blessed Virgin Mary. It was a small beginning but a good one for being open and receptive to the rituals and ceremonies befitting the Sacred Femi9.

Time passes and Daughter of the Rainbow begins to receive guidance and solace in the practice of yoga, chanting and meditation. She had not yet lived twenty years on Mother Earth but she heeded the call. This was the part of the journey that would teach her about the power of stillness. It was quite an enlightening time. With the foundation that she was given, it allowed her to be able to embrace walking the path of a Priestess, surrendering to the countless initiations that she would be taken through.

According to Merriam-Webster's online dictionary, initiation means in part, the rites, ceremonies, ordeals, or instructions with which one is made a member of a sect or society or is invested with a particular function or status. An initiate is being instructed in the rudiments or principles of something. This is an introduction to another way of living and it is not always an easy one. Then again, "It is not what you go through but how you go through it" that makes all the difference in the world.

There are many women who are going through an initiation of some sort. Many of you reading this right now, are experiencing major challenges. The Goddess is pruning you that you may "go to your destiny." Are you willing to surrender to the process?

Your initiation may show you that you are now on a different path than those who are currently in your life. You may experience loss. Maybe the job, that you didn't really like anyway, has come to an end. Maybe the "love of your life" no longer lights your fire and/or attempts to block your progress. You have choices, decisions to make that may not be easy but when you surrender to the process of inner growth you will experience great rewards. Who said life was going to be easy?

According to Sobonfu Some, when a young woman enters womanhood, she goes through a series of events for a period of weeks that tests her resolve. She walks a lot and at certain times is instructed to walk through a rock or jump through the earth, or off a cliff, with guidance, entering a portal, another dimension in order to gain certain knowledge and information to be brought back and used to help the people of her community. Some get lost because they linger too long and the doorway closes for another year. If, at that time, the young woman was not at the right place at the right time, she would be forever lost to her family. Talk about an initiation process!

Amongst those who are initiated Priestesses of a particular Orisha, such as Yemaya or Oshun experience other types of initiations. This way of life originated with the Yoruba of Nigeria. There are countless initiations that go on in various sects or societies, some more intense than others. The common thread of the initiation process is surrendering the ego and letting go of that which no longer serves your highest good.

Daughter of the Rainbow did just that she surrendered to the process of initiation in order to do the work that she was born to do.

11 Ancestral Initiation and the Return of the Ancient Mothers

Ayele Kumari, PhD

Rite of passages are an inherent part of indigenous cultures. They come during times of transitions, growth, and transformation. Typically there are rites of passages when a child goes through puberty, when people marry or become elders. There are other rites of passages that happen when a person called to do healing or spiritual work may undergo. Typically they are performed by priesthood members or other healers in that particular society. These rite of passages are initiations that prepare the individual to become diviners, healers, etc. Recently there has developed a growing movement to bring African Traditions to African Americans that allow for African Americans to be initiated into African priesthoods. These groups are mostly in large cities with heavy African and Hispanic populations. When I was coming of age in my spiritual development, they were not as available as they are now. Even now, many require thousands of dollars and what is given is a title and no training. Early in my spiritual training, I had to rely on the ancestors that had brought myself and my family this far on my journey. They sent me specific women on my path that would be the major trainers in my spiritual initiation. I would become very close to some for a season and others for a lifetime. They formed the core of my spiritual and ancestral initiation. Initiation means to begin and it was them that began me on my journey to spiritual evolution.

It was not long after my coming of age when I realized that I was being taken through an initiation of sorts by my ancestors. My Kemetian ancestors came first, followed by the Ethiopian/ Nubian and then the GaAdangbe ones. Sumerians were another branch that surfaced over time, along with the Omero, and Dakota Souix of the Americas. At one point, I was shown my entire ancestral line and family tree back to the San Khoi in South Africa. I have also come to understand the souls path through reincarnation and the influence of various incarnations that make an imprint on your life. You see, most African Americans are not from one ethnic group. Our bloodlines contain many and date back not just a couple of hundred years, but many thousands. Each mother line and father line have many branches and ancestors may show up from any one or more of those branches. As a soul, you may have incarnated into many more families during your journey on earth.

My ancestral initiation period began in 1990 with my beginning study of the tree of life with a African centered organization. I was 19 or 20 years old and a sophomore at Clark College. The ancients always said that when the student is ready, the teacher will appear. I had searched and searched for something more in the spiritual traditions and had found my first teacher in the Queen Mother in that organization. I learned basic tenants that became the structure for my initiatory period. Meditation, Holistic Health and Natural Healing, Cosmology, Yoga, Astrology, Divination, Ritual, how to work with specific internal divinities and forces of nature, etc. were the basics, but also true spiritual cultivation by elevating your character and self-realization. I took all of the classes that I could and donated as much time there as I could to learn more. I learned how to prepare healthy vegetarian meals by working in the restaurant. I learned to prepare for rituals by assisting with the preparation and eventually setting up shrines. It was a time of tremendous education and training.

Soon I received my first spiritual name after identifying my life's lessons through divination. It came in a dream where I was placed in a circle and several people had their hands on me while chanting it. They were empowering me with the energy. A name is not just a nice sounding word. It is a mantra for your spirit and traditionally reflects your spiritual nature or work. Some people may keep the same name for a lifetime. Others may receive several names as their purpose or focus changes. The custom in that tradition dictated that you would first identify your soul lessons and purpose through divination. Then, someone usually gives you your name after meditation or a ritual. As my ancestors would have it, they gave me my name themselves. I then began to learn the politics of organized religion (African or otherwise) when I went to the Queen mother to tell her that they gave me a name. The original name was Maat Ra Amen. Although it came in Spirit from my ancestors and in a clear dream, she thought that I created the name myself. She told me that I could not have that name because it was the royal family name and I was so new, I couldn't have received it that quickly. I was amazed that anyone would have the audacity to speak against my ancestors but I took the matter back to them. As I fell into trance, they showed my name on a mirror and then marked out the Amen part. They replaced it with Min. I took it to the Queen mother again and she did a reading and accepted it. For years after that, I was known a Maat Ra Min. I was told later that to name a thing can give you power over it so it was necessary that my name did not come from anyone else.

I began dreaming lucidly during the 2nd year of my initiation and that allowed me to maintain my conscious awareness during the dream state. I began to know the people that I encountered by name and recognize them as teachers. One particular one was very old man and had a very long beard. He reminded me of the old pictures people would make of Moses. During my time with him, I became aware of other dimensions and the nature of the universe. I began to astral travel , that is , I was able to leave my body and wander in Spirit form. I found myself participating in ceremonies and rituals that were deep and profound. I also found myself undergoing lessons to obtain certain levels of mastery.

Because of my heavy dreamtime work and interactions in other realms, I was able to receive direct messages that allowed me to delve deeper into my spiritual gifts even without a specific guide on this realm. I was simply given instruction, and I carried the instruction out. I was told what to wear, what to eat, when to eat, when to meditate, and even who I could tell and who I couldn't. I was never asked to do anything that I was uncomfortable with or that went against my personal ethics. I cannot stress the importance enough of never giving your power away. You always have the power to choose your path and you never should do anything that you are uncomfortable with. Initiation is not fear based filled with personal repercussions and ego trips. It is more about soul evolution and training.

The lessons in my personal life became more intense and even focused. The first lessons had to do with caring for my physical body and learning how to better control my emotions and thoughts. Later lessons involved overcoming conditioned behavior patterns that stunted my growth. It was explained that these things were important because they were the first areas of vulnerability that could risk future growth. It was at this time that I was first introduced to flower essences and how they help with emotional/ mental healing.

Once I developed a basic level of this type of skill, I began to become aware of auras, ancestors, and divinities around people. I saw lights everywhere and around people. I also became aware of areas of the body that were dis-eased. This experience was intensified when I began intense training as a healer. In the beginning though, I was just aware of different colors and varying degrees of heat in a particular area.

My third year began with a period of fasting and meditation. I had to fast for 30 days during each season over a year. It always began on the new moon preceding the solstice or equinox for that time. I wore all white during that time and always had my head covered. I cut my hair very short to symbolized a new beginning. I took herbal baths that offered protection from unwelcome and negative energies. During that time I also came across a Senegalese diviner/ healer who gave me a protective pouch to wear around my waist. I was to say as little as possible and my dreams became much more intense.

As the universe would have it, I also found myself working in a temple all its own. I landed a job in the largest metaphysical book distributing company in the world. This company supplied metaphysical and holistic health books to bookstores and companies worldwide. New Leaf distributing company became my temple for higher learning. My study became intensified to maximum speed about everything I could possibly imagine. I developed a vast knowledge of mystical and healing sciences from African mysticism to Zinc minerals. Some of my major interest was in the tree of life, crystals, divination, numerology, astrology, Ancient cultures and civilizations, Christian mysticism, Ancient Egypt/ Africa, esoteric psychology, and anything else I could get my hands on. I also had the privilege to meet many of the authors that wrote those books and I was able to glean personally from their experiences. I know, without a doubt, that I was supposed to be there at that time and to this day, I am grateful for that experience.

My initiation period also entailed some challenges that prepared me for my future spiritual work. Long ago I was warned that some people would see my light and may try to manipulate it to their own advantage. It was during this period of intense growth that I first encountered people trying to do just that. There were elders and priest who presented themselves to me, who in their own right, had already cultivated a certain level of power and reputation in the community. Many came under the guise of friendship and it was only later that I realized they were trying to control me for their own purposes. The lesson of discernment was a deep one and also one where there was some heartbreak because I had become fond of these people and they were elders that I had learned to respect because of their power. It was then that I realized that no matter where an individual may appear on their journey, there are lessons to be learned. I also began to understand how sometimes the student can surpass the teacher. Many of the young ones coming now are far more aware and powerful than my generation and those before me. They are ancient souls returning to earth for a powerful work. It is only our job to teach them what we know and how to use it responsibly. Spirit will take it from there and will awaken their ancient memory as it did mine. They are not ours to control however.

There are two tenants that were repeated to me from various sources during this time. That is Physician, Heal Thyself and Know Thyself. The healer part of my journey came along with a dis ease in my body that had to be healed. In ancient cultures, the most powerful healers had to undergo a test if you will that confirmed their ability to heal. It usually occurred in the form of a condition that needed to be healed. Mine was twofold. One came during this time and the other years later. The first was a condition that was to leave me infertile. I had ovarian cysts and a very bad miscarriage. I had developed endometritis and internal scaring. Although I was only 22 at the time, I was told that I was infertile. They said that my fallopian tubes were blocked.

Although, that was hard to hear, I never believed it. Immediately, I underwent an intense healing regime and self-healing treatment. Acupuncture and massage was a regular part of my treatment. I learned and utilized what I had learned about herbs, homeopathy, naturopathy, energy work, crystal work and others. I believe that the acupuncture was a major component of my healing. I received about 3 months of regular treatment several times a week. I also worked with homeopathic remedies and after both of those, I released a very large clot of mucus and blood. Scared at first, I thought the worst. Later, my ancestors confirmed that it was actually a healing. Two years later, I gave birth to a beautiful baby girl; A confirmation indeed that it had healed.

I encountered a great number of powerful healers and diviners during this period. I came to live with most of them for a time and learned everything from plant identification in my backyard to making spirit pots to fertility rituals. There were 7 major women who were the major contributors to my training each with a different layer of understanding. It is only in retrospect that I could fully see what had taken place. I can only be grateful for all of their contributions to my growth and development as a woman, a healer, and a natural priestess. There was one particular one who over the course of my life has by far been a first a mentor and now a lifelong friend. I met Kuumba during this period and she gave me tools that I still use today. She taught me about the nature of my dreams and visions and how to divine on a much deeper level. She taught me how to integrate what I know and trust it. She also taught me how to keep a light heart through it all. I am so grateful for her friendship and spiritual companionship.

Near the end, I found myself living with a very powerful priestess of the Kemetic tradition. Living with her offered me a period of healing, regeneration, and accelerated growth. By the time I came to live with her, I was exhausted by the trials of the previous year so I was grateful for the reprieve. This woman became yet another spiritual mother and taught me how to harness my power and still remain practical. She taught me how to have my head toward the heavens and my feet firmly on the ground. Firmly armed with all that I had learned, I was ready to stand on my own and live my truth. She taught me the art of massage therapy and hands on healing. She also refined my divination skills and ability to use my magic as a priestess.

My period of initiation culminated in the spring of 1993 at the equinox. I had just completed a 13 day ritual and cleansing. I had a powerful dream on that night in which I was on a beach and waters were running ashore. I was buried in sand with only my head exposed. It was likened to a womb. There were a group of ancestors in white who had shaved my head and made incisions at my crown and in the back of my head. They placed herbal medicine inside the incisions and sealed it up. They began a chant and the waters began to wash ashore eventually covering my head and receding several times. It was frightening and yet they kept singing. Then, the sun came out and I found myself out of the ground and they placed a rub on my body and dressed me in all white. I was given a stone to carry and I was told congratulations because I was finished. That part of my journey was complete and my life would soon change. They explained that I was a healer and teacher and I would share the knowledge of the ancients in this life. They reminded me to keep my faith and remember what I had learned. They also reminded me that I would always be in a state of learning but one day I will lead and teach many others. There was cool wind that breezed across my face and I woke up.

Soon after, I met my husband and had a baby. I trained as a homeopath, a naturopath. .Later I moved back to St. Louis, received a PhD in metaphysical theology and began the work of healing and teaching healing. I have taught over 5000 healers now and have begun the training of women into the tradition of the ancient mothers of the first peoples now re-purposed for the 21st century and planetary healing. Not tied to a specific tradition, but as eclectic as the ancient mothers who guided me, the mixture of ethnic groups African Americans find themselves in, and the ancient traditions that gave birth to the ones we currently know. Within our DNA are thousands of groups, not just one; and our ancestors are many both recent and ancient.

Initiation by the Ancestral Mothers

The year 2005 brought to me a wider awareness and new initiation into the tradition of the mothers. It began as a dream where I was sitting at the base of tree where there were melons growing. I opened one and it turned into a calabash. I took it inside my home and there was a knock on the door. Upon opening it, seven elder women in all white stepped through the door. They carried with them a large star which they said was their emblem. They said they were an ancient

191

sisterhood who had gone underground and was now ready to resurface. They wanted me to join them. At first, I thought they were eastern stars and in a sense they were. These were very ancient women however and not literally associated with the modern freemasonry group. Later I learned that these ancient mothers date back to prehistory and indigenous cultures. They have taken the form of many secret women's societies that were destroyed during the rise of colonialism and patriarchal traditions.

Over the next 7 years, I underwent another initiation...only to the mysteries of the Great mother. It took me on quite a different journey as I awakened to the ancient traditions long forgotten. Many ancient teachings came to me in the night. Often I would wake up and spend days without break channeling the information that I was being given without knowing why it was even important. Suddenly, I could see ancient texts such as the Bible in a totally different light. The pyramid texts became fluid to me and I could hear the ancient mothers ....and fathers guiding me to correct for errors in misinterpretation and translations. It was as if a veil had been lifted and I code read the codes of the ancients quite clearly. In the beginning, they told me I would need to learn more astrology, physics, genetics, chemistry, geometry, numerology, mythology, and so much more. I was extremely intimated as many of these were not my best subjects. Admittedly, I was willing to give up the path when they told me that. Still, each subject was introduced to me subtly at first and then each layer built over the next several years.

This initiation culminated at the equinox of 2012 during the writing of this book and the completion of the DAMO oracle. I was able to see what very few have seen.... the hidden sun and the sacred eye. It is not for me to discuss here, but I will say that this was the last step in ancient priestess initiations. It represents being fully awakened and the culmination of the initiation journey. The journey took 7 years and three major transitions. The first was encountering the Dweller on the crossroads. This was the scariest I must say because one must confront the sum total of all karma from all lifetimes. Again... I nearly quit after that one... The second was encountering your own mortality... death. The third was seeing and merging with the great eye. This is what happened in 2012. The During this time, I heard the music of the spheres and I was congratulated for making it through.

What I have come to understand is something that the ancients would say but I would not comprehend. That saying is Before Enlightenment, We chop wood and carry water... implying the mundane nature of living. Then, After Enlightenment, Chop wood Carry water because while you may now "see" things differently, you are still no different or better than anyone else. You still encounter challenges on the journey not because there is something wrong with you, but because that is just the nature of the journey on earth. However, you know why and you realize your purpose on the planet. You stop seeking "perfection" you realize it is an illusion. You begin to see the illusions. It becomes a matter of just being authentic.

From Girl to Goddess

Now, it is my task, along with many others in their own way, to restore the traditions of the ancient mothers and grandmothers and share this wisdom in the 21st century. The mothers have returned and they are calling their daughters to remember who they are and honor the sacred tradition of the grandmothers. . Goddess consciousness is being awakened, not as an ego trip but as a journey of conscious awareness to release our limitations and conditionings of our humanness and embrace our immortal goddess selves. Take the journey from girl to goddess. Cast off the negative projections of women's power and embrace who you really are. Don't allow other's fear of you to diminish yourselves and your power. It is here to be used to heal ourselves, others, and the planet. As mothers of the planet, we hold the power of creation and restoration of divine order. Honor your dreams for many initiations into the mothers at taking place there. Look around you and notice the great women around you that you are learning from. Whether they are aware of it or not, these are your initiators or co initiators. No man can initiate a woman into her power or confer to her what is her birthright. It cannot be commercialized to control it nor can it be denied if it is your own. The mothers initiate their own in their own way.

It is with reverence that I now call all sisters to reclaim our heritage as daughters of the ancient mothers and of the first peoples on the planet. The original dark mother goddess has returned. It is through our memories that we will restore what was lost, stolen, and forgotten and restore balance on the planet. It is through our reclaiming our power that the world can heal and become whole.

In Honor of the Elder Sisters and Mothers

In closing, I would like to honor of the elder sisters and mothers who initiated my journey, I give thanks for these seven that I learned, laughed, cried, grew wit, each with her own gifts and blessings in my life. I don't even know if they will ever read this or many are now. Our paths have taken many different roads now, all live in different cities and some have crossed over, but all are honored for their unique brand of magic for the time I spent with them.

Ur- Uat Menkt Ur Tau- (Aisha Lumumba)- The Queen Mother who laid my foundation before me. You taught me how to meditate, how to set up a shrine, how to cook vegetarian food, how to use an oracle...and interpret it... astrology, cosmology.... I had my first rituals with you and under your guidance. Thank you for your patience, guidance, knowledge, and wisdom). You ran a business, fed a community in food for the body and the soul...in addition to your own family and sometimes at the sacrifice of them. Others wrote the books, but you nurtured the souls. Thank you.

Kuumba Zuwena- My friend, sister, mother, cousin, mentor, confidant, you taught me the path to healing through your own journey. You helped me find my way, answer the questions, chant my peace, read my cards, listen to my dreams, laugh, cry, heal, yell, fight, and tune in.
You also taught me how to find universal truth in all traditions. You tolerated a million questions from my curious mind and I so appreciate every breath you had to take to answer. I love you always.

Tassili Maat -You taught me how to go in my backyard and find and make delicious food from the weeds, how to be a living oracle, use my creativity and live witty grace and beauty. You opened up my crown with a spiral pattern you braided into my head that was so powerful, it never closed again.

Siam Metut Zulu- You taught me how to work them oracles and my magic pot and listen closely to the ancestors. You also taught me the art of healing. The rituals we did were responsible for ultimately bringing my daughter forth after 2 miscarriages. . After a 60,000 dollar education at Clark, you taught me my real life's work, Massage Therapy, of which I have now taught many thousands.

Amina Gogo Nana- I knew you were a powerful broad the first time I saw you possess HetHeru back in 1990. It was so intense, it scared me. You awakened stuff in me I didn't know I had…. But you danced and massaged my heart with a whole lot of big sister love. You gave me my very first massage… and occipital pull. From you, I learned how to find power in my femininity and many mysteries of womanhood.

Eshua Amen Sa- One of my spiritual mothers. On the other side now but still loved. Living with you every day taught me the art of motherhood and magic. I learned deep trance work and how to bring forth the deities through my person. I learned courage, love, and wisdom. Thank you Ma.

Jakini Auset- I Ching master teacher. The years of talking on the phone, sitting at your feet, and listening to your insights taught me more than I could have ever learned in a class. I learned not just an oracle but how to understand human nature and give loving guidance that evolves the soul.

12 How to Work with the Great Ancestral Mothers

Ayele Kumari Maat, PhD

Working with The Mothers involves developing a relationship with them and cultivating ones divine feminine essence within. The ancestral mothers are a part of every woman's bloodline and in the matrilineal DNA. When we understand that there is no real separation between the living and dead except that we exist in different worlds but can impact each other's world, it makes it easier to understand how the relationship works. It is also important to remember that while we are honoring them and accessing their divine wisdom, we are not worshiping them in the way religions worship an outside entity.

Libations:

Libations is an offering of water, food, or other substance to those on the other side. Its purpose is to energize the spirit body with life force to enable them to have greater impact on the earth plane and thereby assist us in our work. Pouring libations regularly or during ceremony is customary throughout Africa. Offerings such as gin, eggs, cakes, cornbread with honey, wine, bread, fruit, flowers, etc. is also customary for the Ancestral Mothers.

Calling them in:

Libation can begin with a chant or song as well as a ringing of a bell or a drum. Here is a traditional Calling of the Grandmothers and Grandfathers and it is a call and response song.
Poro Mama Ney (Honor the Grandmothers)
(audience repeats)
Poro Mama Neyooo ((audience repeats)
Poro Somo Ney (Grandfathers) (audience repeats)
Poro Somo Neyooo! (All together)

Yo Yo Yo Yo Yooo is another chant that can call in the ancestors.

Next pour your liquid by a tree, a river, or in a plant. A sample libation is as follows... shorten or add as needed. As names are called, call out Ashe as an affirmation and a call of power.

Libation African Goddess

In the name of the Great Mother Divine who comes as
the Goddess within in all forms I call your names:
IyaMi Aje Oshoronga, Mother Creator
Nut, Maat, Auset, Sekhert, Hethert of Kemet,
Sati, Shekmet, Anuke Shu of Nubia
Nana Baruku primordial Mother of the Yoruba
Mami Wata,
Nane Esi, Nana Soonkwa-, Mami Sika, Abenasika,
Asase Ya of the Akan
Abrewa-Primordial Mother of the Akan
Oshun, Oya, Oba, Yemaya of the Yoruba
Ala of the Ibo people,
Minona, Mawu, Gbadu, of the Dahomy,
Dviza of the Shona,
Pomba Gira of South America
Mella of Zimbabwe,
Nowa of the Mende,
Mbaba Mwana Waresa, Amaravi, Inkosazana of the
Zulu
The Shekinah, Holy Spirit, Mary the Mother, Mary the
Tower, of the Hebrew
Kali, Deva, Durga, Ama, Lakshmi, of Indus Kush

In the spirit of our Ancestral Grandmothers, we call
your names
Nzinga: Queen Mother of Angola
Yaa Asantewaa- Queen warior of the Ashanti Nation

Nefert- ta ri   of Kemet
Nandi, mother of Shaka
Makeda, Queen of Sheeba,
Het Shepsu-t of Kemet
Tiye and Kandace of Nubia,

Come forth mothers from the Americas
Harriet Tubman
Sojourner Truth
Madam C J Walker
Mary McCloud Bethune
Zora Neale Hurston
Rosa Parks
Harriet Jacobs,
Phyllis Wheatly,
Ida B Wells,

We call the Big Mamas, the Madias, the Nanas, the Amas, the Iyas, of our mothers, and our mothers mothers,
Dem sistas that plowed the fields, nursed the children, the midwives, the kitchen alchemists who made the worst food taste damn good...
We call the ones who scrubbed the floors, who took the lashes, who lost the babies, who drowned themselves rather than be a slave....
We call on you today, borrow your wisdom, your knowledge, courage, your power, your beauty, you truth, your light

On this day we, as a collective of women, invoke your power. We are seeds of your seeds. Our wombs are from your wombs, we nurture from your breast of life. We bath in your loving grace. We sing in your voices, we pray with your faith, we mother our children as you have mothered us. Ase Speak to us, Guide us forge the path for us, Defend our backs when others come to abuse or destroy us. Open our eyes to have eyes to see. Open our ears to have ears to hear. Open our hearts for true love of ourselves and others.

We give thanks Mama. We give thanks for your DNA. We give thanks for your births, your creations, your earth where we stand. We honor you in our dreams and waking state. You, the mothers of all creation, the queen of queens, the warrior goddess, the portals of death and rebirth, the crossroad guardians, the love weavers, the creatrix, the Matrix, Matter (Mata-Mother). Ase

Creation of an Ancestral Mother Altar

The altar establishes a portal between worlds. Its establishment in your home, yard, or sacred space allows for the energy of the mothers to concentrate and build up so that when you make requests, they can better assist you.

Altars can be outdoors or indoors. Gardens and trees are a great way to honor the mothers. Women have long been associated with the tree and flower of life.

The calabash or gourd is one of the traditional ways the Ancestral mother's energy is contained. The calabash is symbolic of the womb and the world. Within the calabash are all possibilities of existence. Their use with the mothers dates back to time immemorial. Within the calabash, items representing the elements, birds or feathers, red or black earth, stones or crystals, eggs, a drop of blood representing the bloodline and life, may be used. The energy should have a cover on it unless being used to open the energy. Other items that can be used in place of the calabash are pots with tops, jars, bottles, etc. The outside may be decorated as you wish.

It is also appropriate to place water or I like waters from different areas such as ocean, river, lake, etc. Other items such as candles, pictures of ancestors, Sacred Writings, shells and things from the seas, crystals, DAMO Oracles, etc. can be placed on the Ancestral Mother altar.

Celebrating the Ancestral Mothers

The new moon and full moons are traditional times to celebrate, honor, and connect with the mothers. New moon energy is very helpful for healing and releasing as well as planting seeds of intention to be manifested. A healing ritual is one of the best ways I have experienced the use of this energy. Traditionally associated with a woman's menses, the new moon time can be used to heal, pamper, and renew from the stresses of life. Hands on Healing and massage therapy along with crystal, laying on of hands/ Reiki etc. are ideal.

One way to perform the healing is to get a massage table or comfortable chair. One for every 7 or so sister is good. Take turn having each sister in the group sit or lay on the table or chair while the others pray, chant, sing, massage, and lay hands on her. Shower her with loving nurturing energy. Allow her to receive and let go, cry, and open up in safe space and renew. This can also be a time to purify hearts through tears, laughter, sharing challenges and wisdom with one another. Shed old skins of grief, anger, bitterness, and fears. Take turns so that each sister is honored for a time on the table or chair till the work is done.

Full Moon rituals hold great power for manifest. This energy can accentuate anything you are doing. You may align your celebration astrologically or have a specific intention for the participants. Allow yourself to be guided if possible.

Suggested Chants or Chants Honoring the Divine Feminine

Aum Tam , Vam Kling Sah, and Aum Vam Dhum by Ausar Auset Society
Yemaya Asesu or **Ide Were Were** by Deva Premal
Familiar Waters by Sounds of Blackness
Any Chant on the Universal Mother CD by IndiaJiva

Amma- All The While I'm Loving You by Maria Cristina

Holy Spirit, Come and Fill this Place (The Holy Spirit is Feminine energy)

Medicine Woman by Medwyn Goodall

Mother God or Gifts of the Goddess by Karen Drucker

Ocean Music, strings, and flutes are appropriate along with meditation and relaxation music.

These and other songs and traditional chants can be found on youtube to get some ideas.

Above all, allow your intuition to be your guide in honoring the mothers. Also realize that in doing so, you are activating the internal mother source within. This is the part of our being that nurtures and guides our journey in life and creates our world. Honoring the divine feminine helps create our internal insperiences as well as the external manifestation. Honoring the ancestors helps us to connect that which we can see with that which we cannot and provides a channel through which our lives can improve immensely.

Antiquity

Drawing By Dail Chambers

About the Contributors

Alisa Kuumba Zuwena

 Alisa Kuumba Zuwena is both trained and a Natural Intuitive. She has been a reader for over 30 years. She offers transformational consultations for personal growth as well as ancestral readings for those who have crossed over. She facilitates workshops on ancestors, chanting, divination, and more. She is also a visual and performing artist.

Alisa Kuumba's typical Consultations begin with prayer. She uses candles, water, aromatherapy, incense, or other items to promote a positive atmosphere/energy. She tunes into your spirit and tell you what she sees. Many times there may be symbols and/or visions, which she will explain to you in detail. Her decks of choice are the Mother Peace Deck and the Heart Tarot Deck. She may receive direct insight and use further divination to guide her to the answer.

Guidance may be direct instruction, avail options, and may include suggestions to help you with your issue(s). It is best that you take notes from the session so you may reflect later. These readings are completely confidential and private.

Many people ask, "Why should I see a Spiritual/Intuitive Counselor"? Life is full of changes and can often be confusing. Spiritual readings examine or "read" the prevalent circumstances surrounding one's life. The reading can help with decision making and gaining understanding of one's life and particular circumstances.

The areas covered in Intuitive Sessions are relationships, health, career, finances, business and any other are of concern. Yearly and Solstice Readings can be very helpful in exploring issues, areas of needed focus and your theme for a year or 6 months period. Kuumba Zuwena currently lives in Asheville, North Carolina and can be reached at
http://alisasartcreations.blogspot.com/

Priestess Esi

As a Reiki Master, Chakra Healer, Life Coach and Spiritual Healer Priestess Esi, DM is on an amazing journey of learning the mysteries of the Universe.

She has a Bachelor of Science in Biological Sciences - Premedical Studies, she is initiated into the Healing Mysteries of the Universe as a Universal Priestess and is a Doctor of Metaphysics.

Not only is she gifted with the ability to influence energy in order to facilitate healing, but she is also musically inclined. Her instrument of choice is the drum (drum set, djembe, etc), but she also plays the organ and piano. As a musician, she has the gift to heal through music by being a channel from higher realms. The power of the ancestors can be blatantly heard through her drumming.

Priestess Esi always had a passion for health and healing ever since she was 4 years old. At the early age of 11, she affirmed to herself that she is not interested in working with people who have mental and/or emotional issues because those symptoms cannot be measured and those issues can get deep. As she grew in knowledge, she faced the fact that there is a *direct* link between the mind, emotions and body and that disease starts in the spiritual/emotional realm first and then moves towards the physical body if those emotional issues are not resolved. There was a period of time when she was unsure of what healing practice she would use to serve the world; even though she has helped to heal others in the past who had physical issues, she was constantly reminded that she had a strong, POSITIVE impact on the emotions of others. That was the catalyst that sparked Priestess Esi's interest in going on the metaphysical journey into directly linking the emotions with the body.

She continues to expand her knowledge in the area of meditation, herbal and crystal healing, aromatherapy, angelic readings, aura cleansing, goddess energies and the metaphysical causes behind physical disease. Learning never ends and initiation is only the beginning.

If you ever need a spiritual reading, life coaching session, energy healing, to sign up for metaphysical classes or to purchase her album, you can find her at www.priestessesi.com,
www.letthehealingbegin.yolasite.com,
www.queenesi.com www.priestessesi.wordpress.com.
www.eherbalists.com

Tonya K. Freeman

Sensual Womb Shaman Visionary, Motivational Speaker, Pleasure Guide
Affectionately called Diva Mama, Tonya has assisted thousands of women for over 30 years with her transformational work as an Alternative Health Practitioner. She received honorary Doctorates in Divinity, Metaphysics and Motivation from the Universal Life Church and later completed the 10 Moons Calendar Oracle with The Temple of Wombn.

She is vocally vibrant, blending her profound and empowering messages with humor, insight and sage counsel in an entertaining folk wisdom style. Known as *"The Wide Awake Feminine Liberator"*, she has been lovingly referred to as Earth Mother and Global Diva because of her open heart, willingness to share and amazing visionary guidance in helping women realign their natural movement as the powerfully magnetic feminine energy they were born to be.

As a former exotic dancer she discovered the true essence of Diva Energy and later created the *Sexy*

214

Movement and *Diva Danze* classes. She founded *Ladies Personified*, which evolved into *The Art of Femininity*, an online resource for women worldwide. She has contributed articles to Atlanta's *Oracle 20/20* metaphysical magazine and published an online edition of *Spiral Dance News: Unfolding the Femi9 Woman*. Tonya is the co-founder of *Mosa Radio Network*, hosting *Wisdom Talks*, a women's empowerment and wellness program with over 100 interviews in archives and can now be heard on her new talk show *Tonya and Friends*. Recently she has appeared in the film documentary *The Journey of Rena's Moan*.

Tonya's courses, workshops and seminars include:
Womb Magic * *The Sovereign Diva: Victim To Victor* * *Raped Not Ruined* * *Ancient Mysteries For Modern Women* * *Honoring Your Ancestors* * *Come To Me, My Love* * *Naked Confidence: Journey Of The Sensual Soul*

Special Programs:
* *The 30 Day Diva Dialogue*   * *Sexy Spirit Tips*
To book Diva Mama Tonya for speaking engagements contact:

wombshaman@gmail.com
http://awakeningthedivawithin.com
http://tonyakfreeman.com.

Ayele Kumari, PhD

Born as natural intuitive and clairvoyant, she began receiving visions as a child and has continued to do so her entire life. In 1989, she began formal training in the oracles and Kemetian tradition (Egyptian) along with attending college. . Now, she has over 23 years' experience and is highly trained in ancient and modern spiritual technologies, coupled with holistic healing and metaphysics.

She is proficient in astrology, numerology, I ching, tarot, direct prophesy, throwing the bones, cowrie shells along with being a Board Certified Naturopath , licensed in neuromuscular therapy, certified in homeopathy, hypnotherapy, herbology, and 3rd Degree Reiki Master and Seichem Master. She has extensive expertise in ancient history and indigenous sciences. She has a BA in Sociology and Business, an MA in Spiritual Counseling, and a PhD in Metaphysics. She is currently a professor at an allied health college and trained thousands of health professionals in the natural healing arts. While Dr. Kumari experienced an ancestral initiation over 20 years ago, she began intense training in the Women's Mysteries after a life altering dream that introduced her to " The Ancient Mothers" near the turn of the millennium. Her work involves facilitating wholeness in others by helping them to realize their soul's purpose, overcome personal challenges, and heal so that they can empower their life for spiritual awakening. She is also a Maga and Priestess in the Fellowship of Isis, a worldwide priesthood of the Goddess in all forms. During her training there, she was claimed by Shekmet as her priestess but she works toward a unified consciousness of the Goddess within. She offers training and initiations into the Feminine Mysteries and the Ancient Mothers and is founder of Birth of A Goddess, an organization dedicated to promoting goddess consciousness and healing.

She is a mother of 4 adult children and lives in St. Louis, MO. She offers retreats, workshops, online and tele- courses in her specialties. She is also author of Spirit Rising, A Women's Workbook for Healing and Empowerment. She can be contacted through her website, www. Ayelekumari.com

Kajara Assata Nia Yaa Nebthet

 is the founder of RA SEKHI ARTS TEMPLE OF HEALING. She is a Heal Thyself Ambassador of Wellness, Natural Healer, Priestess, Community Activist, Afrikan Holistic Health Consultant, Spiritual Warrior, Sacred Woman, Educator, Mother, who has dedicated her life to promote health, wellness and natural living to our community.

I am a child of SANGO AND SEKHMET sent to this realm to bring light. I am a student of Great African Healers Queen Afua, Dr Llaila Afrika, Dr Sebi, Queen Ayaba Bey, Grandmother Nataska Hummingbird and other great Spiritual Mothers who have helped me remember the Ancient Ways of our Ancestors. I have been a vegetarian for about 19 years, teacher and Mother for 18 years, an artist and craftsperson for 17 years and a spiritualist forever. I worshipped with every spiritual system and searched to find the ways that the first people, the Ancient Ones lived. I became a Sacred Women (thru the Great Mother Queen Afua) and learned about The Great

Healer Sekhmet. It was around this time that I also learned about Reiki. My Spirit was telling me to take some classes and the Reiki class just stood out to me. I became a Reiki Master in 2000

I begin sharing these lessons in the Kemetic tradition in 2007 and have received much more insight about the practice as well. RA SEKHI is the name that was whispered to me to call this ancient healing art, because the practice deals with RA, the Universal Energy that sustains us all and Sekhem, which is our individual Life Force Energy (also called Chi or Ki). Ra Sekhi teaches us to be conscious of connecting our energy to the Universal Energy, being in tune with the Universe.. Ra Sekhi shares how to heal ourselves wholistically using prayers, chants, concentration, focus, symbols, palm healing & natural elements like crystal, oils, incense, and colors as our tools. She promotes health and wellness through classes, events, healing sessions and consultations. For more info visit www.rasekhi.webs.com   , www.youtube.com/rasekhiartstemple or visit her webstore www.niadesigns.etsy.com

Shante "Mama Life" Duncan

Mother, Vocalist, Poetess, Journalist/Activist, Youth Motivation Speaker and Advocate, Grant Writer, Publisher

Shante is a transformational personality and dynamic speaker. She is a passionate social justice advocate who has written articles and/ or edited for several local newspapers, and magazines. She is a free lance journalist/activist (B.A. in Communication from UMSL) and successful grant writer. To date she has played a major role in the procurement of more than 1 million dollars for several local non- profit agencies.

She is founder/chief executive of S.H.E.R.A.H. (Sisters Helping Each Other Reach A Higher Height), a community women's organization created to empower women to assist in the rebuilding of our communities.

She speaks on a variety of topics including:
-Womanhood

-Community Organizing
-Balancing Family and Career
-Natural Family Living
-Personal Empowerment

"Mama Life" believes that mother is her first and most important role as a human being and that mama' is synonymous with teacher, spirit guide and leader. She challenges the notion that men are the natural leaders of tribes, families and households, reminds us to re-examine the role of women in antiquity and advocates for a new and balanced power sharing model especially in our post slavery/ modern circumstance.

She is currently working on a memoir that shares her insights and revelations concerning "growing up in the "Hood", her journey "home to Africa" and her aspirations, thoughts and intentions as a mother and wife.

Shante lives in St. Louis, MO with her husband, daughter and son.

Contact : duncanshante1@gmail.com

www.sherah.webs.com

Dail Chambers

Dail Chambers is a mother, artist and activist who exhibits and lectures nationally. She practices her studio art process in St. Louis Place, in north St. Louis. Her artwork is based in material meaning and women's topics through an inquiry of self and family.

Dail founded the Yeyo Arts collective, a group of five artists who opened Gya, a non profit community arts space that creates arts and culture experiences within the St. Louis region. She has received numerous awards for her work, including a Resolution from the City of St. Louis.

" As creative beings we are constantly moving, pushing, re-evaluating and growing as a process of reflection and progression. Creativity stirs inside of us all. The individual creates, yet it is the community it is gifted for. Our exchange is a vehicle for connecting to one another. We all share this divine urge to create, yet it manifests in beautifully diverse ways."

http://www.dailchambers1.blogspot.com/
http://www.yeyoarts.blogspot.com/
dailchambers@gmail.com

Other Books by Ayele Kumari

Insights from the Priestesses of the Ifa-Orisha Tradition, their Personal Journeys, and Plight for the Divine Feminine

Published 2014

Iyanifa means Mother of Wisdom or Mother of Ifa. It is the

position of the High Priestess in the Ifa Orisha tradition . The Ifa Orisha tradition of Africa is thousands of years old and was so strong, it was able to survive the slave trade to go on in the new world. What didn't survive the slave trade ,but remained in Africa was the position of Iyanifa. In a world where women have lost much of their ancient mysteries to patriarchy and slavery, a tradition is presented here that went underground but did not die. Iyanifas, Iyami, and Queen mothers of Africa resurface now to continue a legacy for new generations across the globe. This book is a collection of stories, essays, and explorations of the position of Iyanifa and its resurgence in the Diaspora. Gleaned from the perspective of the elder mothers who broke the glass ceiling to reclaim the tradition , they share their divine wisdom teachings, candid personal experiences, joys, and growing pains drawn from their lives as Iyanifas and women in the tradition. This volume of work features authors such as Luisah Teish, Iyanla Vanzant, Aina Olomo and many other powerful healers, diviners, and counselors. It is offered as a gift to women in the tradition and to those interested in Woman's and African Studies to explore the path of Iyanifa and to be a resource for years to come.

Ayele Kumari, PhD

Spirit Rising

Women's Workbook for Healing & Spiritual Empowerment

Published 2010

Part Memoir, Part Magic, Part Medicine for the Soul! Spirit Rising is blend of memoir from hard life lessons, along with practical tools for personal healing and spiritual

225

empowerment. From challenges such as rape, molestation, abandonment, suicide, teen pregnancy, Kumari shares personal stories on not only how to survive, but will give you specific tools to transcend it all. As she navigates you through the path of spiritual freedom you will uncover hidden mysteries within through exercises, journaling, and activities. Utilizing ancient spiritual technologies and timeless wisdom, she will take you on a journey to wholeness in your life. Through applying these ancient sciences, you will gain answers and assistance to challenges such as emotional healing and breakthrough solutions to personal challenges. Through learning how to understand the nature of spiritual laws, you will learn how to identify your soul's purpose, along with monthly and yearly themes that will help you maximize your opportunities. Many will tell you to change you to change your thinking and you can change your life. This book will tell you how to do it along with giving you tools for everyday guidance that can give you insights into your finances, relationships, and life.

Made in the USA
Monee, IL
23 June 2020